THE RETURN

Barry Chant
and
Winkie Pratney

Sovereign World

Sovereign World,
P.O. Box 17,
Chichester PO20 6RY
England

All scripture quotations are from the New International Version
unless otherwise stated, © 1973, 1978 International Bible Society.
Published by Hodder & Stoughton.

ISBN 1 85240 026 9

Printed and bound in Great Britain by
Anchor Brendon Ltd, Tiptree, Essex

Contents

Hallelujah! He is coming again!
Christ is coming back again!
Sing hosanna, He is coming to reign,
Christ is coming back again!
Israel's King will soon be here;
David's crown He will wear.
Sing hosanna, He is coming to reign,
Christ is coming back again!

INTRODUCTION

In November, 1977, the President of the United Arab Republic of Egypt, Mr Anwar Sadat, made a historic journey to Israel where he talked with the Prime Minister, Mr Menachem Begin in an effort to resolve conflict in the Middle East. Both men were subsequently awarded the 1978 Nobel Prize for Peace. The American President, Mr Jimmy Carter strongly supported these initiatives. A couple of years later, a Christian pamphlet appeared which claimed that this meeting was a clear indication that the return of Christ was about to occur any moment. The reasons? Simple.

It was now sad at Jerusalem and this was the beginning of sorrows. The other day, I heard of a group who believed that Christ would establish His kingdom in Florida, because the divine name (I Am) formed the central three letters of the word 'Miami'. In Australia, there is a credit card called Bankcard. Its logo features the letter 'b' in three colours. The shape of the 'b' is not unlike a '6'. Many people have suggested that this card represents the mark of the beast! (When Visa Card appeared it had a silver dove, with subtle rainbow tonings - was this a sign of the Holy Spirit?)

One of the greatest human achievements in the world is the Great Pyramid in Egypt. It is truly awe-inspiring. Many books have been written suggesting that the Pyramid is actually a divine monument in which the length of the passages, if measured out in inches, mark off the years of human history. Several dates for the end of the age have already been passed. Since the end of the passage ways has now been reached, some pyramidologists seem to be going up the wall.

In 1986 and 1987, a certain brightly dressed gentleman was a regular figure at Speakers' Corner in Hyde Park, London. He claimed he was William Tell, reincarnated as Jesus Christ.

All of these examples indicate some of the many fascinating, astounding, funny-sad ideas that may be found concerning the return of Christ and the end of the age. One preacher recently referred to it as 'comic book theology'!

On the other hand, there are those who don't believe in such things at all. When one man was told that we were working on a book on the second coming, he was incredulous. 'You mean the sort of thing Jehovah's Witnesses talk about? I didn't know you believed in it.'

Then there are those who say that biblical teaching about the return of Christ is only another way of talking about death. When you die, that is the second coming for you.

Others say Jesus was referring to the descent of the Holy Spirit at Pentecost, when He spoke of His return.

Then there are those who believe that biblical teaching on this subject is just a poetic way of describing how the world will eventually become Christianised.

Who is right? Fortunately, there are many good books on this issue and there is a sound, informed body of thought which represents a general consensus among conservative thinkers. Unfortunately, even within this area, there are still fairly major differences of interpretation, and even more unfortunately, some writers would have us believe that their's is the only acceptable view.

In this book, we have tried to do two things. In the first part, we have set out the major truths of the return of the Lord that we feel almost everyone will agree with! You will see that there is a great deal of straight-forward, clear, plain teaching on the subject in the Bible, about which, as far as we can see, anyway, there is little room for variance. Perhaps we are too optimistic! Nevertheless, we do not see how any reasonable Bible reader can avoid the conviction that Christ will return to the earth in power and great glory and that we need to be ready when He does. And this is essentially what the first part of the book is about.

In the second part, we have looked at some of the more contentious issues, and tried to present several alternatives. No doubt, our own views will show through fairly clearly - in fact, we haven't really tried to hide them. But we also want to acknowledge that there are alternatives held by good and reputable people and that we respect them, even if we don't agree with them.

This book is really designed for the everyday reader. You don't need to be a scholar to know what we are on about! On the other hand, we hope that serious students of Scripture will also find much to think about in what we have to say and maybe even use this short volume as a text.

'Behold, I am coming soon!'
Amen. Come, Lord Jesus.
(Revelation 22:7, 12, 20)

PART ONE

The plain teaching of Scripture explained by Winkie Pratney and Barry Chant

Chapter 1
Why Christ Must Return

'…What will be the sign of your coming and of the end of the age?' (Matthew 24:3)

What does the future hold? The disciples of 33 A.D. were not the only ones down through history who have wanted to know! The subject of future prediction is one of the major obsessions of our time. Futurology is in; science fiction books are best-sellers and future-set movies are massive box-office.

Astrologers, spaceage sooth-sayers and New Age channelers all figure high on the interest list for talk shows and autograph parties. With Michael Fox it seems we're all going 'Back To The Future' - coming 'nuclear-fuelled, time-junction capacitor-equipped DeLorean, ready or not'.

Why must Jesus return? Because He *said* He would, and He is a God Who cannot lie. 'Prophecy on His coming is the subject of some 1,845 verses of the Bible, 318 of these in the New Testament. It is the dominant theme of 17 Old Testament books and one epistle in the New' (John Westley White, 1971, p.14).

When Jesus came the first time, prophecy was fulfilled in awesome detail; and He, the Sovereign Lord of history said He would come again.

Jesus will return. It was the vision of the early apostles; it gave them dynamic and direction.

It is the teaching of all the great creeds of the Church; in the Apostles Creed, 'He shall come to judge the quick and the dead'; in the Nicene, 'He shall come again with glory'.

Martin Luther said, 'I live as though Jesus Christ died yesterday, rose again today and were coming tomorrow.' Tyndale's motive for ministry was 'Christ and His apostles warned us to look for Christ's coming every hour.' Bishop Ridley, burned at an Oxford stake for his witness, cried as he died: 'Come Lord Jesus!'

Charles Wesley appealed to Christ's return as the climactic goal of all Christian service, including the theme in 5,000 of his 7,000 hymns. Jonathan Edwards' writings on the Second Coming inspired founders of many early mission societies like William Carey, Henry Martyn and Alexander Duff, and later William Patton and David Livingstone: they believed a pre-condition of Christ's return was that 'this Gospel of the Kingdom shall be preached in all the world for a witness to all nations; then shall the end come' (White, 1971, p.25ff).

When Jesus answered his disciples that day He gave them *nine major signs* of the 'birth pangs' of a 'last generation'. While scholarly opinions may differ whether or not that generation meant those listening to Him then (see Chapter Four for a fuller discussion on this), what He said then still strikes a universal chord in the hearts of people today. We find our world in a very similar situation to the one Jesus described to His disciples.

1. World War

> You will hear of wars and rumours of wars, but see to it that you are not alarmed. Such things must happen, but the end is still to come.
>
> (Matthew 24:6)

The first sign Jesus mentioned was a pre-occupation with war. In Jesus' day, Rome had conquered most of the known nations: it had brought universal transport, communications and global peace to the then-known world. With the dissolution of the Empire, wars broke out afresh, and have been such a feature of modern civilization, that if a visitor from some alien world closely observing us had to report back on our chief interests and industries, he would probably conclude that beside sex, entertainment and drugs, it was chiefly *war*.

> Then another horse came out, a fiery red one. Its rider was given power to take peace from the earth and to make men slay each other. To him was given a large sword.
>
> (Revelation 6:4)

War is a multi-billion dollar industry and the cost each year keeps jumping. In Caesar's day it cost 75c for the Roman Army to kill an enemy soldier. By World War I, it had risen to $15,000; by World War II, it was $30,000; in the Korean War it cost $50,000; and in Vietnam over one million dollars! (White, 1971, p.44).

Related also to this sign of the last days is not only wars, but 'rumours of wars' a continual *awareness* of war; now possible for the first time in history by a system of world-wide satellite communication links.

The communications revolution (which involves satellite, television, fibre optic and information processing technology such as computing) has not only integrated much of the world to a common consciousness, it has also made it possible for the first time in history to link the diversity of nations with a common control.

In what Toffler calls our 'Information Age', *inform-ation technology* is the coin of the realm and, as one analyst fondly hoped in the early '70s, 'The computer, in short, promises by technology a Pentecostal condition of universal understanding and unity. Electricity will exorcise social disorder and environment disruption, eliminate political conflict and personal alienation, and restore ecological balance and a communion of man with nature' (John Rasmussen, 1972, p.30).

If any generation has felt the power of this apocalyptic threat it is this one: Big Brother's children. Prince put it like this in his hit album *1999:*

> I was dreamin' when I wrote this
> Forgive me if it goes astray
> But when I woke up this morning
> I could have sworn it was judgement day
> The sky was all purple
> There were people runnin' everywhere
> Trying to run from the destruction
> And you know I didn't even care
>
> Cuz they say: 2000 zero zero party over oops out of time
> So tonight I'm goin to party like it's 1999
> > (Prince: *1999,* Controversy Music,
> > ASCAP, 1982, Warner Bros)

Young people used to be afraid of the dark; now they are afraid of a terrible light. One of the great fears young people have today, other than that of losing their family or close friends, is *world-wide nuclear destruction.* It is the constantly-recurring theme in punk, underground speed-, black- and heavy-metal music.

All modern kids today grow up with a conscious

knowledge of the power of 'the Bomb.' When 'Fat Boy' was detonated in the sky above Hiroshima on August 7, 1945 the world changed. Mr. Ripley of Ripley's 'Believe It Or Not' said from the ruins of what had been one of Japan's most beautiful cities, 'I am standing on the spot where the end of the world began.'

Over 80,000 people died instantly; within 36 hours, another 120,000 died as the infection and suffering became so great they gnawed out their tongues in pain. But the first bombs were tiny (20 kilotons: equivalent to 20,000 tons of TNT) compared to what we have now.

The heart of a modern thermonuclear detonation is a heat core one hundred million degrees Fahrenheit - both silent and visible radiation travelling at the speed of light. It can so instantly vaporize clothing, flesh and bone, that running civilians, caught by the Hiroshima blast in the open, left only their shadows burned against what was left of the walls.

Then the shock wave travelling at the speed of sound; and the blast, collapsing buildings, spraying stone, wood and glass, like a myriad of lethal fragmentation grenades. An awesome firestorm sucks out all air within the blast area, leaving nothing to breathe. And then finally, the fallout; dropping back from 70,000 - 12,000 feet up, lasting, lingering radioactive poisons that leave the ground sterile and pollute food and water.

But modern ICBM's can each deliver impacts of 25 *megatons - over 1,000 times more powerful* than the bombs dropped in Japan. Missile-carrying subs can have 16 missiles, with up to 14 multiple independently-targeted warheads, each equal to some 60,000 tons of TNT, Just *one* of these subs could destroy any country on earth. Russia has reportedly tested a 100 megaton bomb - 33 times more destructive than all combined explosives used during the entire six years of World War II!

Prince again echoes the feelings of frustration and fear of so many kids who think 'since nothing I do can stop the end of the world, I might as well go out feeling good'

> I was dreamin' when I wrote this, so sue me if I go too fast
> But life is just a party and parties weren't meant to last
> War is all around us my mind says prepare to fight
> So if I gotta die I'm gonna listen to my body tonight
> I got a lion in my pocket and baby he's ready to roar
> Everybody's got a bomb we could all die any day
> But before I'll let that happen I'l dance my life away
> Mommy … WHY does EVERYBODY have a BOMB?

Is there a bomb in Gilead? When the Bible speaks of final war it sets it right back in the Middle East.

Why should the Middle East be such a centre of world attention and tension in the last days? For centuries no-one cared. Now even in major secular novels, the Middle East figures centrally on the opening scenarios for World War III, because of its single most important economic asset: oil. Projected world oil production peaks about 1995, and by 2015 it will have dropped by half.

With world economics deeply affected by oil production prices, the risk or world war centering around the Middle East becomes more apparent every day. ('Red Storm Rising' Tom Clancy?). The Middle East has become a central military focus; it contains not only over 53% of the known oil reserves of the world, but the chemical deposits of the Dead Sea, estimated to be worth trillions of dollars; it also forms the only land bridge between Europe, Asia and Africa.

2. Spiritual War

And kingdom against kingdom ...
They overcame him by the blood of the Lamb and by the word of their testimony; they did not love their lives so much as to shrink from death.

(Revelation 12:11)

A theme that shows up less in the reality of statistics but more in the fantasy life of the young is their hunger for *militancy*. You see it in the martial arts videos kids buy in the stores; the popularity of the 'Commandos', 'Mad Maxes', 'Robocops', 'Rambos' and Rambettes (Sigourney Weaver in 'Aliens') and the continuing popularity of fantasy adventure gaming. 'Violence,' said Karl Menninger, 'once used to be a last resort. Now it is a means of communication.'

'Enemy-occupied territory,' said C.S.Lewis, 'is what this world is. Christianity is the story of how the rightful king has landed, you might say landed in disguise, and is calling us all to take part in a great campaign ...' *(Mere Christianity,* 1952, 1986, p.51). No wonder fantasy war gaming has become a major interest amongst the young; they are conscious that the ultimate war is spiritual, and that the real battle is not with flesh and blood, but with spiritual wickedness in high places.

17

3. Famine

> I looked, and there before me was a black horse!
> Its rider was holding a pair of scales in his hand.
> Then I heard what sounded like a voice ... saying,
> 'A quart of wheat for a day's wages, and three
> quarts of barley for a day's wages, and do not
> damage the oil and the wine'.
>
> (Revelation 6:5,6)

Here the Bible speaks of famine so bad, it costs a man his entire pay packet for enough food to feed his family for a day. Whatever affects one nation, affects the prices of all commodities; and food and water are the basic needs.

Whenever God seeks to get the attention of a nation that refuses to heed His word, His first resort is to 'break the staff of bread'. The economies of nations are as vulnerable to the dealings of God as the fortunes of an individual.

In 1970, the Volkswagen Foundation granted $250,000 to an international team of scientists to study survival. 'The Limits to Growth' report chart included known natural resources, population growth rates and pollution. Depletion of natural resources and population growth were plotted against time, and their conclusion was that 'all growth projections end in collapse' before 2020.

Now the Club of Rome report was pessimistic, totally humanistic and deeply flawed; but the reality of daily starvation peers at us from haunted, ghostly eyes, in heads that sit on bloated bodies, with matchstick legs; people are dying by the thousands every day, and nothing seems to be able to check the vicious cycle.

In 1975 Gordon Rattray Taylor stated, 'The fact is,

the long-prophesied world famine is here' *(How To Avoid The Future*, p.258) 'And what do you want to be when you grow up little girl?' asks an adult to a child. 'Alive.'

Bob Geldorf, ex-lead singer of the Boomtown Rats, unintentionally became an internatonal celebrity for his efforts in uniting rock musicians around the world, to focus attention on world hunger. 'Band-Aid', 'Live-Aid' and other related concerts have highlighted for many people what Christian ministries like World Vision and Tear Fund have sought to bring to public notice for decades; too much of the world is dying of hunger.

Two thousand years ago, before anyone foresaw it, and before anyone really cared, Jesus said it; the world as we know it now would suffer from starvation. It will be one of the signs of His coming and of the end of the world.

4. Earthquakes

Of all natural disasters, there are few as unexpected and frightening as an earthquake. There has been a measurable upswing in both the frequency and intensity of earthquakes monitored over the past five centuries. In the 16th century they recorded 153; in the 17th, 378; in the 18th, 640; in the 19th 2,119. In the 20th there have already been more than during the last 5,000 years!

And the more severe earthquakes are increasing. Last century there were six. In this century there have been over 35 major earthquakes (most with towns 89%-100% destroyed, as in Guatemala in 1976, and all with terrible devastation, as in Mexico City in 1987). 'During recorded history, earthquakes - and the fires, floods and landslides they have triggered - are estimated to have taken as many as 74 million lives.' *(Time,* September 1, 1975, p.50).

Yet some recent Christian studies suggest the original earth may have been designed to last *indefinitely;* at its core was a perfectly balanced breeder-reactor furnace, modulating warmth through a water shell to the surface. At the time of the first destruction of the world, that balance was shattered by the spoken Voice of the Judge of the world, and the outer granite-soil layer of landmass cracked like a microwaved egg.

Now earth's core is a molten furnace under great stress, and recent measurements of its internal temperature are higher than those taken previously. The continents pull precariously away from each other, creating stresses that can only be resolved by violent shifts of the land-mass.

> I watched as he opened the sixth seal. There was a great earthquake. The sun turned black like sack-cloth made of goat hair, the whole moon turned red, and the stars in the sky fell to earth, as late figs drop from a fig tree when shaken by a strong wind.
> The sky receded like a scroll, rolling up, and every mountain and island was removed from its place. Then the kings of earth, the princes, the generals, the rich, the mighty, and every slave and every free man hid in caves and among the rocks of the mountains.
>
> (Revelation 6:12-15)

I was in a major earthquake in Los Angeles in 1971 that hit shortly after 6 a.m. It began with a deeply disturbing feeling (subsonic vibrations) and then suddenly, violently and audibly, the walls shook, things fell down and people all over the L.A. Basin began to scream. If it had not been still quite dark and almost windless I would have thought the city had just been hit by an atomic bomb.

I turned on the radio and a local D.J. had just picked himself off the floor to grab the mike again. 'My God!' he said, 'It was just like a giant hand swept everything onto the floor!' I thought it significant that the first thing he said was 'God', and the analogy he used was of an invisible hand. I thought of Belshazzar and the words of the stunned magicians of Pharoah - 'This is nothing more than the finger of God', and suddenly I had a whole new picture on the power of the judgement of God.

The most devastating thing I remember about it was the feeling of *total physical insecurity*. We rarely realize what a sense of confidence solid ground gives to everyday life. When the ground itself shakes, all confidence vanishes and there is no place to hide. We trust the ground. We expect it to stay firm. It is utterly shocking and unsettling when it moves like a live thing.

I felt for days afterward like a man on a hammock, hanging over a cliff with one end unwinding. My stomach muscles would not relax. It was hard to sleep for many nights afterwards because you were never sure that the numerous little after-shocks were not preludes to the 'Big One' still to come.

5. Persecution

Then you will be handed over to be persecuted and put to death, and you will be hated by all nations because of me ...

(Matthew 24:9)

21

When he opened the fifth seal, I saw under the altar the souls of those who had been slain because of the Word of God and the testimony they had maintained. They called out in a loud voice, 'How long, Sovereign Lord, holy and true, until you judge the inhabitants of the earth and avenge our blood?'

(Revelation 6:9,10)

With the Church seen as the last great bastion of absolutes and righteousness on earth, all perceived representatives of Christian religion become the target of destruction:

Hang the Pope
Hang the Pope ...
Hang the Pope
Hang him with a f---ing rope
... Lets go to the Vatican
Get him out of bed
Put the noose around his neck
And hang him till he's dead'

('Nuclear Assault' from Game Over,
Combat Records, 1986)

And again from 'Slayer', billed as the 'fastest and heaviest metal band in the United States' -

The Holy Cross, symbol of lies,
Intimidate the lives of Christian born
Speak of death, the words of hate
Anticipation grows amongst the dead
Hell has seen the priests attempt
To bring forth the Lord of the cross
Strike of twelve, raise the dead
The chapel comes under attack ...

The church now belongs to the dead

Blackened magic infest with lust
Lucifer reigns supreme ...

Ghosts from Hell invade this feeble shrine
Heaven's holy house will fall in time
Satans morbid soldiers chant in lust
Destruction of the church we'll burn the cross

Attacking angels as they pray to God
Tormented preachers hail the twisted cross
Haunting the chapel hell's demons prevail
Death has come the house of God has failed
('Haunting the Chapel' from the album by
'Slayer', 1984, Metal Blade Records)

6. **Apostasy**

At that time, many will turn away from the faith
and will betray and hate each other ...'
(Matthew 24:10)

But mark this: There will be terrible times in the
last days. People will be lovers of themselves,
lovers of money, boastful, proud, abusive, disobedient to their parents, ungrateful, unholy,
without love, unforgiving, slanderous, without
self-control, brutal, not lovers of the good,
treacherous, rash, conceited, lovers of pleasure
rather than lovers of God ...
(2 Timothy 3:1-4)

People feeling cheated, disappointed and dissatisfied with society have not only a sense of helpless-
ness but, as Taylor has said more fundamentally, 'the
inexplicable need to find an *over-riding purpose* in life

... There are three classic ways to relieve such existential anxiety: sink oneself in a *project* - political, charitable, artistic or even the struggle for personal prestige and public honors. The second is to *live for the moment,* extracting maximum pleasure from every sensory or emotional experience. The third is to *prepare for life in another world;* in a word, to turn to religion. No doubt today we need a new religion - it would have to be a matrist, orgiastic one, modelled on the worship of Ishtar and Cybele. ... You cannot build a constructive society with destructive people, a peaceful society with violent people or a civilized society with uncivilized people (G.R.Taylor, pp.280-281).

Especially does this feeling of hopelessness and powerlessness erupt among the young -

> I fight a losing battle now to keep myself controlled
> But it seems like no-one cares I'm about to lose my soul
> Selling that which God gave me for a price of gold
> To travel freely into Hell has become my goal
>> ('Sin: Nuclear Assault': from *Game Over,*
>> Combat Records, 1986)

7. Religious Deception

And many false prophets will appear and deceive many people ...

(Matthew 24:11)

Having a form of godliness but denying its power. Have nothing to do with them. They are the kind who worm their way into homes and gain control over weak-willed women, who are loaded down with sins and are swayed by all kinds of evil desires, always learning but never able to acknowledge the truth ...

(2 Timothy 3:5-7)

At that time, if anyone says to you, 'Look, here is the Christ!' or, 'There he is!' do not believe it. For false Christs and false prophets will appear and perform great signs and miracles to deceive even the elect - if that were possible. See, I have told you ahead of time.

(Matthew 24:23-25)

What is *the key sign of the last days?* Jesus said it would be *religious deception.* In all the discussions about the signs of the last days, the 'sign of the fig tree' figures prominently.

Now learn this lesson from the fig tree: As soon as its twigs get tender and its leaves come out, you know that summer is near. Even so, when you see all these things, you know that it is near, right at the door.

(Matthew 24:32-33).

The unique thing about fig trees is that they are the only trees in the Bible where the fruit appears before the leaves. And as Arthur C. Custance points out, the fig tree is an analogy not of the *spiritual* (the olive) or *political* history of a nation (the vine), but its *religious* history. In God's purpose, there must always be fruit before leaves, reality before religion, and the chief sign of the last days is a blossoming of the religious.

Jesus warned us about the last days. He said there would be terrible deception and that its final form would be *religious* and *miraculous.* It would claim idenitity with God. It would claim Messianic purpose, and produce its own paranormal wonders as documentation. The final consciousness to rule the world before Jesus returns will be something very like the scenario developing in our times.

> For the time will come when men will not put up with sound doctrine. Instead, to suit their own desires, they will gather around them a great number of teachers to say what their itching ears want to hear. They will turn their ears away from the truth and turn aside to myths.
>
> (2 Timothy 4:3,4)

8. Lawlessness

> Because of the increase of wickedness, the love of most will grow cold
>
> (Matthew 24:12)

What is 'lawlessness'? The word not only implies contemptuous disregard for God's law (and by implication all law) it involves flagrant defiance of the very *idea* of law, an amorality that publically flaunts evil as normality. Lawlessness can come from two extremes: the lawlessness of a *cynical carelessness* (not believing in a returning Christ, the Judge of the whole earth) or the lawlessness of *hopelessness and abandonment* - a nihilistic fatalism about the end of the world.

The lawlessness of the head-banging thrash metal groups of the fringe underground is the lawlessness of abandonment; an 'aselgia' of shameless conduct, the deliberate and flagrant flaunting of evil that comes from no hope and no mercy, as 'Possessed' make plain on their album *Seven Churches* -

There's a sacred city not far from here
Where the earth is bare and the sky is black
Tormented souls are stricken with fear
And the sinners all know there's no way back ...

Fly into the Pentegram
There's a lot you'll want to see
Sacrifice the crying ram
And drink the blood with me ...
You can't escape your destiny
So take my hand and fly
To an evil land of fantasy
Inside Satan's eye ...

('Pentagram' by 'Possessed' from *Seven Churches*, Combat Records, 1985)

As John Whitehead points out, crime has increased exponentially in our generation, especially amongst the young. In America, child crime of a serious nature (aggravated assault, rape, robbery, murder) rose a staggering *11,000%* between 1950 and 1975! *(The Stealing of America*, 1983, p.68).

The second facet of this sign is *apathy* - 'the love of many will grow cold'. Again there are two kinds of apathy; the apathy of *carelessness* and the apathy of *hopelessness*. The first rules amongst the parents, and the second rules amongst their children. In the 60's they knew all the answers, but didn't know the questions; in the 80's they are bombarded with so many questions they don't even want to think of the answers.

William Booth pointed out a century ago that the greatest dangers of the 20th Century would be religion without the Holy Spirit, Heaven without Hell, faith without repentance, salvation without Lordship, and Christianity without Christ.

9. World-Wide Evangelism

And this gospel of the kingdom will be preached in the whole world as a testimony to all nations, and then the end will come.

(Matthew 24:14).

What is the key condition awaiting fulfilment before the end? The message of God's rulership over the individual, the family, the church, the city and the nation must be taken into the whole world.

I watched as the Lamb opened the first of the seven seals. Then I heard one of the four living creatures say in a voice like thunder, 'come!'

(Revelation 6:1)

The great commission in our generation? David Barret, editor of the ground-breaking *World Christian Encyclopaedia* (1982) has begun an ongoing communications project, with a view to world missions and evangelism. (The 'AD 2000 Series': New Hope P.O. Box 11657, Birmingham Alabama 35202-1657). These studies seek to sum up both current global conditions, and future projections in the mega-cities and unreached people groups of the world.

He is quite confident that with the data we presently have in hand, the task of the Great Commission *could literally be completed in our lifetime.* He suggests a realistic and realizable goal of 'discipling all nations' is to plant at least 100 new disciples in each of 1,000 unreached ethnolinguistic peoples, and by evangelism produce at least two congregations in each by A.D. 2000.

Evangelism, the other side of the Great Commission

is 'not just speaking or preaching, but proclaiming Christ with full authority and power. Signs and wonders accompany the evangelical message' (Kittel). To fulfil the commandment 'this Gospel must be preached … for a witness', we would need to evangelize some 1,741 million untouched people by A.D. 2000, Or 116 million a year *(318,000 a day)*.

Present efforts are close; combined global ministry touches around 300,000 new people a day! Both the evangelization of the whole world, and the discipling of all nations is a very real possibility in our generation.

The dawn of the New Twentieth Century witnessed the greatest missions movement of history. Barrett points out that by 1900, not only were all of the largest five cities on the world (London, New York, Paris, Berlin and Chicago) centres of Christian mission, witness and dicipleship, but close to 70% of urban dwellers in the world were Christians! (World-Class Cities and World Evangelism, p.10).

A large portion of this thrust can be traced to the expectancy of a new century and a conscious sense of Jesus' Second Coming. As Phillips Brooks said during that time: 'The coming of the Lord has been the inspiration of the Christian world. The power of any life lies in its expectancy.'

But with the Twentieth Century came not only massive population increases in cities of Third World countries, already centres of non-Christian world religions, we also reaped the consequence of inadequate preaching and teaching. Concurrent with the rise of evolutionary thought and liberal theology, the return of Christ received bizzare and unbalanced treatment, first at the hands of its would-be friends, and then at the hands of its skeptics and its enemies.

The world stopped looking up for a Saviour. With

W.E. Henley it declared, 'I am the master of my fate; I am the captain of my soul.' It took two World Wars and the threat now of a Third for the pendulum to swing back again.

Now the topics of Christ's Second Coming, the Kingdom of God and its implications to the world, form probably the single most significant area of study, discussion and debate in the Christian church today; and whatever the conclusions drawn, this one thing is sure: the world as we know it is right out of hope. Its humanistic well has just about run dry, and the ground-swell of ordinary people are hoping for a Messiah.

It is the hidden hunger behind the rise of the New age movement and the fantasy explosion; we need someone to come who cares and is both wise enough and powerful enough to help us out of the mess we have got ourselves into. There are, to be sure, Messiahs a-plenty and Christs not a few; but gone are the days when any old bearded-and-sandalled pretender to the throne could announce his coming to be The Coming.

No, if you are going to be noticed at all, you will have to do better than Guru Maharaji (the former teenage aspirant to the throne of heaven) whose Houston appearance was modestly billed as the 'Greatest Event In The Universe'; or the not so subtle Benjamin Krim world-wide newspaper announcements 'The Christ Is Now Here'.

If you are going to capture the attention of a media-weary, 'Believe It Or Not', 'That's Incredible' world, you had better have something that at least looks like the real goods. Or as He said - *be* the Real Thing.

Jesus must come. He said that in the last days 'many would come' in His Name. The long line, the procession of imposters is becoming more and more embarrassing and more and more bizzare. He will not put up with it much longer. Jesus will come. He said it, and we can stake our future on it.

Chapter 2
Why Christ Will Return

The return of Christ is promised throughout all of the Bible. In fact, it is one of the major biblical themes. In both Old and New Testaments, there are multiplied promises that Christ will come to establish His kingdom on the earth.

When Jesus came to this world the first time, many of His contemporaries thought that the Old Testament prophecies about His second coming in power were to be fulfilled then. This is why there were attempts to make Him a political leader.

He alone saw that His first coming was to be in suffering and pain for the sins of mankind and that He would come again a second time in power.

This He made very clear, for example, on one occasion when He tried to explain to His disciples that He was about to be taken by the religious leaders of the day, tried and crucified. Peter took Him aside and said, 'Never, Lord! This shall never happen to you!' (Matthew 16:22).

But Jesus told Peter plainly that he was talking from a human point of view - he couldn't see things from God's perspective.

Jesus knew that His suffering was inevitable - indeed, this was the very reason why He had become a man. He would be killed. But He would also be raised again from the dead!

Then Jesus went on to make a further important point. Not only would all these things happen, but there was a day in the future when the world would see

Him again - 'For the Son of Man is going to come in His Father's glory with His angels, and then He will reward each person according to what he has done' (Matthew 16:27).

On that day, He would not come as the suffering Servant, but as the reigning King! The angels whose aid He refused at the cross (Matthew 26:53) would now be at His side to enforce His rule!

In this way, the Lord made it clear that just as He had come to earth the first time, so He would come again a second time. The difference, however, would lie in the manner of His coming. Not in lowliness, but in exaltation! Not in obscurity, but in glory! Not in weakness, but in power! Not in sacrifice, but in supremacy! Not in meekness, but in majesty!

When we look at the Old Testament promises of the coming of Christ, we must draw a distinction between those which speak of His coming as Saviour, and those which speak of His coming as Sovereign.

Passages like this clearly refer to His role as Saviour -

He was despised and rejected by men,
a man of sorrows and familiar with suffering.
Like one from whom men hide their faces
he was despised and we esteemed him not.
Surely he took up our infirmities
and carried our sorrows,
yet we considered him stricken by God,
smitten by him, and afflicted.
But he was pierced for our transgressions,
he was crushed for our iniquities;
the punishment that brought us peace was upon him,
and by his wounds we are healed.
We all, like sheep, have gone astray,
each of us has turned to his own way;

and the Lord has laid on him
the iniquity of us all.

(Isaiah 53:3-6)

There is no doubt that we have here a prophetic picture of the Lord Jesus Christ suffering for our sins. Isaiah wrote these words some 700 years before the death of Christ. Yet they so accurately depict exactly what happened at the cross. There, Jesus died for us. Although we were the ones who had strayed from the paths of integrity, our waywardness and selfishness and resultant punishment was laid on Christ!

On the other hand, there are many passages which talk of the Lord's return to earth in power. Many of these can be identified by the occurrence of the phrase 'the Day of the Lord'.

In general terms, this expression refers to any day of judgement or any visitation from God. Joel uses it, for instance, to describe the devastation caused by an unprecedented locust plague (Joel 1:15; 2:1ff). Similarly, Amos describes the eighth century B.C. invasion of the merciless Assyrians as happening on the day of the Lord (Amos 5:18,20).

Many times, however, the Old Testament prophets talk about that day in such graphic and universal terms, that it cannot be limited to a local event. They clearly have in mind an age-ending, cataclysmic intervention by God in the affairs of men. This is confirmed by the way in which New Testament writers also talk about the Lord's return as 'the day of the Lord' (eg see Phil 2:16; 1 Thessalonians 5:2; 2 Peter 3:10).

There are several extensive passages in the book of Isaiah, for example, which are presented in this vein.

In the second chapter, Isaiah declares that the Lord Almighty has a day in store on which He will bring judgement on all who are proud or arrogant. Using the metaphorical language so typical of the prophets, he describes even towering trees, high buildings and tall ships as being brought down! As for men, they will try to hide in caves and under rocks in terror and 'from dread of the Lord' (2:19,21).

'The arrogance of men will be brought low,' says the prophet, 'and the pride of men humbled; the Lord alone will be exalted in that day' (2:17).

So great will be the impact of the Lord's presence that the very earth will shake!

In the third chapter, Isaiah goes on to say that the finery and jewelry of the women will be snatched from them, and they will be ashamed and embarrassed.

Finally, however, the Branch of the Lord will be 'beautiful and glorious' in the land. Other passages make it plain that this is a reference to the Lord Jesus Christ, the Messiah, who is a righteous Branch from the family tree of Jesse (Isaiah 11:1ff; Matthew 2:23, where Matthew may also be using a play upon words in that the Hebrew word for 'branch' is similar to the word for 'Nazareth').

This statement is in sharp contrast to the other prophecies in Isaiah that Jesus would be despised and rejected, and that He would hold no attraction for those around Him, as happened at His crucifixion. 'On that day', however, He will be very different. This time He will appear in His true beauty and splendour. Moreover, He will cleanse and protect His people and His glory will be their canopy (Isaiah 4:5).

There are many other passages in Isaiah which talk of the return of the Lord (eg 11:10f; 13:9-22; 65:17ff). Perhaps the most outstanding is the last chapter in the book.

See, the Lord is coming with fire

36

and his chariots are like a whirlwind ...
For with fire and with his sword
the Lord will execute judgement upon all men,
and many will be those slain by the Lord ...
'And I ... am about to come and gather all nations
and tongues and they will come and see my glory ...
'...the new heavens and the new earth that I make
will endure before me,' declares the Lord.

(Isaiah 66:15ff)

This passage shows the last great day of God when He will rule over all the nations and establish His everlasting kingdom.

Joel also speaks of such a day. As we have noted already, the prophet initially uses the phrase 'day of the Lord' in reference to a great locust plague in his own time. But he does more than this. In fact, the invasion of locusts becomes a prototype of the Lord's wrath at the end of the age. The very language he uses about the locusts indicates this, when he refers to them as a great army, and talks of the earth shaking before them, and the sky trembling.

But it is in Joel's third chapter that he specifically describes age-ending events. Here he speaks in strident tones of all the nations of the earth gathering together to do battle. Then, however, the Lord sits in judgement upon them because of their great wickedness.

Multitudes, multitudes
in the valley of decision!
For the day of the Lord is near
in the valley of decision.

(Joel 3:14)

But then, the Lord will save His people and protect them so that they will never again suffer invasion or harm. There will be everlasting prosperity.

In that day the mountains will drip new wine,
and the hills will flow with milk;
all the ravines of Judah will run with water.
A fountain will flow out of the Lord's house ...

(Joel 3:18)

How much of this is to be taken literally, is a matter of question, of course. It is obvious that at least some of the language used is symbolical (eg 'the hills will flow with milk'). But it is equally obvious that the scope of the events described is universal and eternal, not local and temporal. In other words, these are events that mark the end of an epoch.

The prophet Amos who was, like Joel, a contemporary of Isaiah, also speaks of a final establishing of God's kingdom.

And he also uses the phrase 'day of the Lord' in a local sense initially (5:18,20).

But like Joel, he goes on to talk of final things as well. 'In that day', he says, 'the Lord will restore the people of God and establish them for ever' (Amos 9:11-15).

Similarly, Micah talks of a day when there will be universal peace, and the law of the Lord will be followed universally. Swords will be beaten into ploughshares and spears into pruning hooks, and 'every man will sit under his own vine and under his own fig tree' (4:2-4). In other words, instruments of war will be re-fashioned into tools of agriculture, and each individual will be economically sufficient.

It is the seventh century prophet Zephaniah who highlights the concept of the day of the Lord. In proportion to the length of his short book, this is a prominent theme.

The great day of the Lord is near -

38

near and coming quickly.
Listen! The cry on the day of the Lord will be
bitter,
the shouting of the warrior there.
That day will be a day of wrath,
a day of distress and anguish,
a day of trouble and ruin,
a day of darkness and gloom ...

(Zephaniah 1:14ff)

Like Isaiah and Amos, Zephaniah warns that the
day of the Lord will not be all sweetness and light. For
many it will be an occasion on which they wish they
had never been born.

Indeed, Zephaniah goes on, the whole world will
come under the fire of God's wrath (1:18).

Nevertheless, on that day, there will also be re-
joicing, for the Lord will be there with his people,
'mighty to save', and He will rejoice over them with
delight, with love and with singing.

Moreover, sorrow, sickness and shame will be
removed for ever, and God Himself will gather His
people together (3:19f).

While some of these Old Testament prophecies do
not specifically refer to the return of Christ, they do all
speak of the consummation of the age, and the ushering in of the kingdom of God.

When we read the New Testament, we discover that
the same phrase ('the day of the Lord') is used of
Jesus' return. So we can safely assume that the Old
Testament prophets were talking of the same event.

There are prolific predictions of the return of Jesus
Christ in the New Testament. Our Lord Himself and
His followers all spoke of it in plain, certain terms.

Jesus promised that He would return to the earth a

second time. In the next chapter we will look at the nature of this return and the things that will happen then. At this point, it is enough to see how often Jesus and his followers declared that He would come again. It is also interesting to note the absolute certainty that all the New Testament writers show when they speak of the Second Coming.

Our Lord Himself put it as plainly as it is possible for words to express. 'I will come again,' He said (John 14:3). And on another occasion, 'Yes, I am coming soon' (Rev 22:20).

One of His most important discussions with His disciples took place on the Mount of Olives, not long before His death. Among other things, they talked of the end of the age and what would happen then. At that time, Jesus told them, all nations would 'see the Son of Man coming on the clouds of the sky with power and great glory' (Matthew 24:30; Mark 13:26; Luke 21:27).

He went on to make repeated references to His coming, and to the need for us to be ready for it (eg Matthew 24:36,42, 44; 25:13). And again, he spoke of the day when He would come 'in His glory, and all the angels with Him ...' (25:31).

Similarly, on another occasion, the Lord declared that the day was coming when all the dead would hear his voice and be raised from the grave (John 5:25-28).

It is impossible to read the teachings of Jesus honestly and objectively, without believing that He promised to return to this earth a second time. He made it very clear.

Christ's teaching was confirmed in a very dramatic way within moments of His ascension to heaven. On that very day, two men in white suddenly appeared with the overawed disciples. They, too, spoke very plainly of Christ's return. 'This same Jesus, who has been taken from you into heaven, will come back in the same way …' (Acts 1:11). Words could not be clearer.

The apostle Paul has much to say on the subject as well. Again, we shall return to Paul's teaching in more detail later. But even a cursory glance makes it clear that he believed in and expected the Lord to return to the earth.

To the Corinthian Christians, he used phrases like 'when he comes' (15:23) and 'he must reign' (15:25) and 'the dead will be raised' (15:52).

To the Philippians, he spoke plainly of the day of Christ (1:10) and told how eagerly he was waiting for the Saviour to return from heaven (3:20). He encouraged his readers to rejoice, to be gentle, not to be anxious - because 'the Lord is near' (4:5).

Paul's greatest emphasis on the Second Coming is in his two letters to the Thessalonians. Phrases like 'when he comes' (1 Thessalonians) and 'he will come' are used repeatedly (eg 1 Thessalonians 2:19; 3:13; 4:14-16; 5:2). In plain terms, Paul says, 'he will appear' (2 Thessalonians 1:7-10).

Similarly, Paul writes to his young protégé Timothy about all those who long for Christ's appearing, (2 Timothy 4:8) and to Titus about the 'blessed hope' that we have in the return of Jesus (Titus 2:13).

The writer to the Hebrews likewise points out that just as Christ appeared once on the earth to take away sins, so He will appear a second time (Hebrews 9:28). Similarly, James exhorts his readers to be patient 'until the Lord's coming' (James 5:7-9).

Peter, too, firmly believed that Jesus would come back to earth. He encourages the believers to stand firm until the time when the Lord would be revealed (1 Peter 1:7), and says very clearly that 'the day of the Lord will come' (2 Peter 3:10).

41

John warns us to abide in Christ lest we be ashamed before Him at His coming (1 John 2:28). And Jude says simply, 'The Lord is coming with thousands upon thousands of His holy ones' (Jude 14).

Finally, the Book of Revelation is devoted to the theme of God's ultimate plan for the universe and the consummation of this age through the return of Christ.

> Look, he is coming with the clouds,
> and every eye will see him,
> even those who pierced him;
> and all the peoples of the earth will mourn
> because of him.
> So shall it be! Amen.

(Revelation 1:7)

There are many other specific promises of the second coming of Christ in this book, often in symbolic language. So He is described as the Son of Man seated on the clouds, with a gold crown on His head and a sickle in His hand, ready to reap the world's last harvest (Rev 14:14ff), or as a rider on a white horse proceeding in victory (Rev 19:11ff).

Finally the book concludes with the establishing of the kingdom of God and the thrice-repeated promise, 'Behold, I am coming soon!' (Revelation 22:7,12,20).

There can be no doubt that the Bible abounds in promises of the return of Christ. This is the great hope of Christians. We have the clear guarantee that things will not drift on aimlessly to despair and destruction. History is not haphazard. From eternity to eternity God has a master plan. This plan is centred in and accomplished through the Lord Jesus Christ.

So Paul declares that God has an 'eternal purpose' which He is realising through Christ (Ephesians 3:11). The second advent is an integral part of this strategy.

In 1984, I was in South Africa. There were many at that time who were despairing of any kind of answer to the racial conflicts and tensions of that beautiful land.

My purpose in being there was to attend the dedicatory services for the huge 34,000-seat tent that had been commissioned by the German missionary-evangelist, Reinhard Bonnke, of Christ for All Nations, (CFAN).

This tent, the largest moveable structure of its kind ever made, was a great symbol of hope in a troubled land. One member of the CFAN team was a black singer named Tommy Saaiden. He sang at the dedication banquet, and again at many of the meetings in the great tent. One of his most popular songs went like this -

> He's coming soon, there's no doubt,
> I'm going to leave this old world with a shout!
> Sin will be gone and things will be right,
> Keep looking up, He may come tonight.
> It may be in the morning,
> It may be at noon,
> I don't know when He's coming,
> But I know He's coming soon!

This simple song reflected the ultimate hope of people everywhere, especially those in South Africa. Not that they were not trying to do something here and now. They were. Genuine efforts were being made to redeem lives and hence society from prejudice and hatred. But ultimately, they knew there was only one lasting solution to human mismanagement of God's good earth - and that was to hand the oversight back to Him.

In the person of Jesus Christ, God visited our planet and walked among us nearly two millennia ago. He will do the same thing again one day - this time not in human frailty, but in divine omnipotence.

He will return. He said so.

Chapter 3
How Christ Will Return

On October 22, 1844, thousands of people in the United States waited prayerfully for the return of the Lord Jesus Christ. Many of them had disposed of their properties, resigned their jobs and settled their accounts. Any moment, they expected Jesus to burst through the clouds and to appear like a lightning flash across the sky. Nothing, of course, happened.

They returned to their homes, disillusioned and disappointed. William Miller (1782 - 1849), an effective preacher who was welcome in the pulpits of Protestant churches of all persuasions, was the man who had built up their expectations. He was now discredited. The event is commonly referred to as the Great Disappointment.

Some of Miller's followers, however, went back to the drawing board and decided that Miller had been right in his calculation but wrong in his interpretation of his date. What happened was that Christ began the investigative judgement of mankind on that day, a process that would culminate in His final return in power. Out of that group came the Seventh Day Adventist movement.

In more recent years, in Sydney, Australia, a zealous group of believers actually built an ampitheatre where they could gather to welcome the Lord at His return.

Another nineteenth century American to attract an enthusiastic following was Charles Taze Russell (1852 - 1916). According to him, 'the times of the Gentiles' (Luke 21:24) concluded in 1914, a view, incidentally, which has been shared by others as well (eg Foster, *Antichrist,* p. 41; Guinness, 1880, p. 671 - Guinness differs from Russell by about ten years).

Russell's followers eventually became known as Jehovah's Witnesses. They came to the conviction that 1914 would also be the date of the Lord's coming. Some fifty years later, a Jehovah's Witness publication stated -

> The King arrived in His glory in AD 1914. He sat down 'on his glorious throne'. So it is now, during this 'time of the end' that the King separates people ... goats on his left ... sheep on his right ... Soon now the time of the end will close ... Many are the people alive since 1914 who will still be living when it is time for Armageddon to begin. In 1914, Jesus was crowned King of the new world ...
>
> (*Paradise Lost: Paradise Regained,* pp.200ff)

For a long time after 1914, Jehovah's Witnesses used the slogan, 'Millions now living will never die!' As the years have passed, however, that cry has been heard less and less.

It is very obvious that there are many different ideas about the nature of the second coming! Speculation about what will happen when Christ returns is widespread. However, there are enough plain statements in Scripture for us to be quite clear about the essential factors involved.

Our Lord Himself spoke freely on the subject and so did the apostles, in particular, Peter and Paul.

Before reading this chapter, it could be very helpful for you to read the following passages from the Bible -

Matthew chapters 24 and 25

Mark chapter 13

Luke chapter 21

1 Thessalonians chapters 4 and 5
2 Thessalonians chapters 1 and 2
2 Peter chapter 3

A sound working knowledge of these significant New Testament passages will give you a strong grasp of the subject. In fact, I would suggest that you not only read them, but make notes of the major points and then try to organise your notes into a systematic order.

By the time you have done all that, you probably won't need to read the rest of this book! However, perhaps you should continue, if only to compare notes! I should point out that while there are many clear concepts presented in the passages concerned, there are also some quite difficult ones (eg 2 Thessalonians 2:7, which has baffled its readers for centuries). Don't let the difficult ones detract you from assimilating the clear ones, however. Unfortunately, this has happened more than once. So we have extensive debate on infrequent, obscure passages, at the expense of clear teaching on the plain truths.

So why don't you put this volume aside right now and take out your Bible?

* * * * *

Well, how did you go? I'm sure you found the teachings of Jesus and His apostles thought-provoking, stimulating and encouraging. And I'm also sure that you have many questions in your mind about some aspects of what you read. Hopefully, your questions will be answered by the time you reach the end of this book.

For instance, what did Jesus mean when He said that 'this generation' would not pass away until everything he spoke of was fulfilled? Who is the 'lawless one' spoken of by Paul? How do we interpret the signs of the end of the age? What is the great tribulation? And is there any clue at all to what Paul means in 2 Thessalonians 2:7?

All of these issues will be picked up as we go along. However, we want to look at those areas about the second coming which are clear and plain.

At this point, it might be helpful to mention a couple of Greek words which are used to describe the coming of the Lord. These words are *parousia, apokalupsis* and *epiphaneia*. Each of these expressions conveys a different aspect of the Lord's return. While they all refer to the same event, the varied nuances in meaning help us to understand it more fully.

There have been suggestions that these words refer to differing stages of the second advent. However, when we look at their usage in the Bible, we find that they are simply alternative names for the same event. Each word does bring out a different emphasis, however.

To take the last one first. *Epiphaneia* is only used by Paul and it only occurs about four times. Its literal meaning is 'appearing' but it also has connotations of the idea of 'brightness'. It was used in Greek mythology of the glorious manifestation of a god, especially when coming to someone's aid.

It is in this sense that Paul uses the word. He talks about the *epiphaneia* of Christ's coming - that is, the brilliant appearing that will form its essence (2 Thessalonians 2:8). He writes to Titus, the overseer of the church at Crete, of the 'blessed hope - the glorious appearing of our great God and Saviour, Jesus Christ' (Titus 2:13). Again, the use of the word implies brilliance and splendour.

It is interesting to note, however, that *epiphaneia* is also used of Christ's first coming and in particular of

His resurrection - which revealed, in a similar way, His glory (2 Timothy 1:10).

The next word is *apokalupsis*. The derivation of the English word 'apocalypse' from this word is obvious. Its essential meaning is 'to reveal'. It is used in many different ways in the New Testament - the name of the last book in the Bible derives from it, for a start, and it is the word generally employed for any kind of divine revelation (eg Ephesians 3:3).

Luke gives us one example of Jesus using it to describe His return (Luke 17:30), and both Peter and Paul talk of Christ being 'revealed' when He comes again. The suggestion is that when the Lord does come back, it will be obvious to all.

The other word *parousia* is the most commonly used. It means 'presence' or even 'arrival', especially of some important person. So it might be used in reference to a king or ruler whose arrival back in his territory is greeted enthusiastically and ceremoniously by his subjects. It was also used to describe the beginning of the reign of a new emperor in New Testament times. In Corinth, for example, special coins were struck in honour of a visit by Nero - or in other words, a *parousia*.

Paul uses the word in reference to everyday events like the arrival or *parousia* of Titus (2 Corinthians 7:6f). On another occasion, he warns the Corinthians that he will be just as strong in his *parousia* as he is in his absence (2 Corinthians 10:11).

So when we speak of the *parousia* of Jesus Christ we speak of His arrival on earth once again, as He returns like a long-absent ruler, literally to make His presence felt among us! Jesus Himself used the word frequently in His Olivet discourse, and most of the New Testament writers make it their most common name for the second coming (eg 1 Corinthians 15:23;

1 Thessalonians 2:19; 3:13; 4:15; 5:23; 2 Thessalonians 2:1,8; 2 Peter 1:16; 3:4,12; 1 John 2:28). In fact, it has also become anglicised, and it is not unusual for modern writers to talk about the Lord's parousia.

It can be easily seen that all three terms refer to the one event. Paul talks, for instance, of the *epiphaneia* of Christ's *parousia* (2 Thessalonians 2:8).

In summary we can say that the words used by the New Testament writers make it clear that their understanding of the second coming, is of a time when Christ will be revealed in brilliant majesty, as He arrives once again among us, personally present.

Of course, the common verb for 'come' is also used frequently of the Lord's return.

Now let's look at some of the major features of the parousia of Jesus Christ.

First of all, the Lord will return personally. - Everything about Jesus' teaching makes this clear. Although He avoided personal pronouns and preferred to refer to Himself as the 'Son of Man' or 'your Lord', He clearly spoke of Himself as a person who would come again as a person. So He used parables comparing Himself to a householder (Matthew 24:45ff), or to a bridegroom (Matthew 25:1ff), or to a property owner and investor (Matthew 25:14ff).

The householder, for example, comes home personally. He does not send a representative. So when he does return, the steward he has left in charge is caught without excuse. Similarly, the investor does not send a messenger to see how things are going at home. He himself returns, to review the success of his staff in their use of the talents which he has entrusted to them.

And as for the bridegroom, he could hardly send another in his place!

There is no doubt that Jesus expected that He Himself would return to the earth a second time, personally. As we have noted, His use of the word *parousia* also indicates this.

At His ascension, the angels said to the disciples that 'this same Jesus' would return (Acts 1:11). Paul confirmed this when he wrote that 'the Lord himself' would descend from heaven (1 Thessalonians 4:16).

Secondly, the Lord will return publicly. There will be no secret about it! Again, Jesus Himself made this crystal clear. Consider the following extract from his discourse with his disciples on the Mount of Olives -

> For as lightning that comes from the east is visible even in the west, so will be the coming of the Son of Man...
> At that time the sign of the Son of Man will appear in the sky, and all the nations of the earth will mourn. They will see the Son of Man coming on the clouds of the sky, with power and great glory. And he will send his angels with a loud trumpet call, and they will gather his elect from the four winds, from one end of the heavens to the other.
>
> (Matthew 24:30ff)

This description leaves no room for the idea that Christ might return invisibly, anonymously or surreptitiously. When He comes, all the nations of the earth will know about it and will see Him coming. Language could hardly be plainer.

Some might argue that Christ was talking in metaphorical terms and that He did not expect to be taken literally. While this is undoubtedly true of some of the statements of the Old Testament prophets, and of the Book of Revelation, it does not seem to apply to this passage. In fact, it reads rather like a newspaper report - except that it is news written in advance! And where imagery and word-pictures are used, they seem in obvious contrast to the rest of the passage. For example, Jesus does use both simile and metaphor in his reference to the vultures gathering to a carcase (Matthew 24:28), and the fig tree sprouting (Matthew 24:32f). But these are clearly different in style from the rest of His language.

Similarly, Paul describes the Lord as returning 'with a loud command, with the voice of the archangel and with the trumpet of God' (1 Thessalonians 4:16). These terms, even if taken metaphorically, can only apply to a very public event. Shouts and trumpet calls are hardly appropriate for something secret!

The writer of the Revelation puts it simply when he says, 'every eye will see him' (Revelation 1:7). You can't be more public than that!

The New Testament presents a very graphic picture of the Lord Jesus Christ appearing in spectacular and dramatic fashion in the heavens. Like a brilliant electrical storm, whose lightning flashes span the skies and illuminate the whole landscape, and whose thunder claps rebound from horizon to horizon, so will His coming be.

Some people have suggested that the satellite television network now encircling the globe will enable every nation to see Him at the one time. In this way, they say, the Scriptures can be fulfilled. I doubt it! Christ will come in such splendour and power that He will have no need of any invention of man to help Him achieve His ends. His divine glory will be more than enough to touch all nations at one moment of history, and to fill them all with awe and despair at His arrival as King of kings and Lord of lords, President of presidents and Ruler of rulers, Governor of governors and Prime Minister of all ministers!

Let us make no mistake. When Jesus Christ comes again, there will be no secret about it!

Thirdly, He will come powerfully. This is why all the nations will mourn when they see Him. They will realise the feebleness and frailty of human resources when they are confronted by the power of the Almighty.

The incredible power of Christ's coming is suggested strongly by the language used. The shout and trumpet call indicate military strength. It is traditional for armies going into combat to raise their voices to try and intimidate the enemy. Whether we think of Red Indians, Zulu warriors or modern soldiers on a bayonet charge, the noise of battle is a common factor. Today's explosives add a further dimension.

Nowadays, of course, we don't sound the trumpet to launch an attack, but for thousands of years, this was the common method of rallying troops for battle. It does not matter whether there will be a literal trumpet sound at the second coming. There will be a literal rallying cry of some kind, a call to arms, a sky-piercing, heart-thrilling summons that will be heard by every living creature in heaven and on earth! Christ will be present in power.

Also, Jesus will be accompanied by myriads of angels (Matthew 24:31; 1 Thessalonians 4:16; 2 Thessalonians 1:7). Jude says there will be 'thousands upon thousands' (Jude 14). In fact, all the angels of heaven will be involved (Matthew 25:31). It will be a display of divine power and majesty unprecedented in history. No wonder the nations will mourn!

At this point, we must recognise our need to dispense with the traditional, rather effeminate concepts of angels that many people have. Angels are not just inoffensive, mild creatures, who spend all their time playing gentle harps on heavenly clouds, their golden wings glowing in the sunlight. They are powerful servants of God, ministering spirits whose role is to serve

53

His people (Hebrews 1:7, 14). Just one angel was able to destroy a whole army in one night (2 Kings 19:35). Angels are awesome beings.

As we go on, we shall see further details of how the power of God will be displayed at the return of Christ. It will be the most powerful, dramatic, earth-shaking event ever experienced by mankind.

We can gain a glimpse of what could happen, by considering some of the huge catastrophes of nature. For all the horrific destruction that humanity has been able to cause through weaponry, especially in recent years, we are still sorely limited in comparison with the immense power of an earthquake, a tidal wave, a volcanic eruption or even a bush fire. When the forces of nature are unleashed, we are like ants before them.

Similarly, when Jesus Christ returns to the earth, there will be nothing that can even begin to resist His power. It will be as awesome as an earthquake, a tidal wave, a volcanic eruption, a cyclone and a flood all rolled into one!

All the nations will be in terror before Him.

Fourthly, Christ will return to gather His people to Himself. One of the roles of the angels will be to 'gather his elect from the ends of the earth to the ends of the heavens' (Mark 13:27). In this way, the people of God will join their Lord to fulfil their eternal destiny in His everlasting kingdom.

Paul also writes of 'our being gathered to him' (2 Thessalonians 2:1). In his first letter to the Thessalonians, he gives some specific details about how this will happen. First of all, there will be the resurrection of believers who have died (1 Thessalonians 4:13ff). Because of this, he says, there is no need for us to mourn and grieve as others who have no hope. Just as the Lord Jesus died and rose again, so

God will bring back from the dead with Him all those who have 'fallen asleep'.

In fact, the Greek expression used here could imply the idea of Jesus rising from the grave and then leading all those who trust in Him in a great procession behind Him. It is a vivid picture of a great pageant of victorious believers ascending to heaven as Jesus 'brings them with Him'.

> The Lord will descend with a shout and the trumpet call of God and the dead in Christ will rise!

Paul gives some detailed teaching about the resurrection from the dead in his letter to the Corinthians. First of all, he points out that without hope of resurrection, the Christian faith is pointless. In fact, if there is not resurrection for us, then Christ was not raised from the dead either - the whole thing is a myth. Both stand or fall together. Either Christ was raised and we, too, will be raised, or Christ was not raised and neither shall we be (vv 12-19).

Next, Paul uses an analogy from the harvest. Just as in Old Testament days, the 'firstfruits' of the crop were presented to God as an offering (Leviticus 23:10ff), so 'Christ has indeed been raised from the dead, the firstfruits of those who have fallen asleep' (v.20). Then, like the rest of the harvest, all those who belong to Him will also be raised to life 'when he comes' (v.23).

The apostle also uses martyrdom as an example of the certainty of resurrection. In those days, when many Christians were being put to death for their faith, others were coming forward to be baptised and to take their place. Ironically, the more that the believers were persecuted, the more the churches grew. Nearly 200 years later, the great Christian lawyer Tertullian was to write, 'The oftener we are

mown down by you (ie the Romans), the more in
number we grow; the blood of Christians is seed'
(*Apology*, 50).

Why, asks Paul, should these new believers be
baptised in the place of the dead, if the dead are not
raised? What is the point? (vv 29ff). (Incidentally, this
passage has nothing to do with baptism by proxy, as
the Mormons practise.)

Thirdly, Paul anticipates the question, 'How are the
dead raised? With what kind of body will they come?'
(v. 35). Again, he answers this with an analogy from
nature. A seed that is sown is never the same as the
plant that grows from it. It is put into the earth in one
form and emerges in a very different form.

So it will be with the resurrection of the dead. The
body that is sown is perishable, it is raised imperishable; it is sown in dishonour, it is raised in glory; it is
sown in weakness, it is raised in power; it is sown a
natural body, it is raised a spiritual body (1 Corinthians 15:42-44).

There is no doubt that the resurrection will be
physical. We will not be disembodied spirits wafting
around the skies. We who are raised from the dead,
will be raised bodily. The oldest creeds of Christen-
dom have affirmed this (eg the Apostles' Creed). But
the bodies in question will be very different from those
we now have.

Even now, the human body has a sense of divine
glory about it. It is a masterpiece of creation that in-
spires awe and admiration. But in that day, it will be
even more glorious. It will have a new kind of
splendour. It will be imperishable; it will be glorious;
it will be powerful; it will be spiritual; it will be im-
mortal (vv. 43f, 53f). In simple terms, it will be like
the resurrection body of Christ! (v. 49; Philippians
3:21).

In his delightful volume, *The Great Divorce,* C.S. Lewis describes a bus trip from hell to heaven! Astonishingly - yet perhaps not so astonishingly, when you think about it - the people concerned don't like heaven when they get there! Among the many aspects that they find unpalatable is that everything there is so real. The blades of grass cut their feet; the water from a waterfall is so strong, they cannot put their hands in it; a daisy is so steel-like that they cannot pick it; and even a leaf is so heavy that it cannot be lifted from the ground.

And as for the inhabitants of heaven, Lewis calls them 'solid people'. In contrast, those on the bus are just 'ghosts' -

I saw people coming to meet us ... The earth shook under their tread as their strong feet sank into the wet turf ...

Some were naked, some robed. But the naked ones did not seem less adorned, and the robes did not disguise in those who wore them the massive grandeur of muscle and the radiant smoothness of flesh. Some were bearded, but no one in that company struck me as being of any particular age ...

They came on steadily. I did not entirely like it. Two of the ghosts screamed and ran for the bus. The rest of us huddled closer to one another.

As the solid people came nearer still, I noticed that they were moving with order and determination, as though each of them had marked his man in our shadowy company ...

(1946, 1986, pp.29,30).

I do not know of any more profound a statement in English literature of the nature of the resurrection body than this. The popular idea, of course, is exactly opposite. Most people think of heaven as being an insubstantial, wispy place, with white clouds and golden haze, and generally useless people playing harps all day. Lewis gives us a far more biblical concept: that of true reality.

Both Paul and the writer to the Hebrews tell us that this earth and the things in it are but 'shadows' of the ultimate reality to come (Colossians 2:17; Hebrews 8:5; 10:1). So our present bodies will seem like weak reflections of the true bodies that we will have.

Moreover, this will not only apply to those who have died. True, when they are raised, they will be renewed. But living believers will also be changed. By-passing the door of death, they will enter immediately into the same resurrection realities.

> And all this will happen in a moment, in a flash, in the twinkling of an eye! When that last trumpet sounds, heralding the coming of the Lord, the dead will be raised and we shall all be changed!

> (vv. 45-54)

What a dramatic event!

The Lord Jesus also talked about this during His time on earth. 'The time is coming,' He said, 'when all who are in their graves will hear his voice and come out - those who have done good will rise to live, and those who have done evil will rise to be condemned' (John 5:28,29).

At the same time, living believers will also be caught up to meet the Lord. Remember how Jesus said that He would send his angels to gather His elect? Paul says something similar in 1 Thessalonians. After the dead are raised, living believers will be 'caught up together with them in the clouds to meet the Lord in the air' (1 Thessalonians 4:17).

Just how this will happen, we do not know. If we take the words literally, we have a picture of people rising physically from the ground, in defiance of gravity, and ascending like substantial balloons to meet the living Christ.

There can be no doubt about the significance of the event, however. From this time on, all believers, whether previously living or dead, will be with the Lord forever.

No wonder Paul exhorts us to encourage each other with these truths!

This great event is commonly known as 'the rapture', from the Latin word *rapto* which means 'I snatch', and which suggests the idea of God's people being 'snatched' out of the world. Certainly, this is the great hope of believers in Christ. Whether we die or whether we live, we know that the day is coming when Christ will reign over the earth, and that we will live forever in harmony with one another and with Him!

Not only will the Lord return to gather His own people, but *He will also come in judgement on those who have rejected Him.*

Whether we like it or not, this is a major theme throughout the Bible. In the Old Testament, in particular, this aspect of the second advent stands out. We have already noted how the prophets used the term 'day of the Lord' in reference to the parousia. Although they saw this day as being followed by an era of everlasting peace and prosperity, the day itself was not one to look forward to - as Amos said,

> Woe to you who long for the day of the Lord!
> That day will be darkness, not light...

(Amos 5:18)

In order to emphasise the gravity of such a time, Amos draws a vivid picture of a man who meets a lion and flees for his life. No sooner does he think that he has escaped the lion than he is confronted by a bear.

59

Finally, he manages to reach his house in safety, leans against the wall to catch his breath - and is bitten by a snake! (Amos 5:19).

In this way, Amos shows the inevitability of God's judgement. On that day, there will be no escape!

The New Testament writers also describe the time of Christ's return as 'the day of the Lord' (eg 1 Thessalonians 5:2; 2 Peter 3:10). Sometimes, just 'the Day' (eg 1 Corinthians 3:13; Hebrews 10:25). And when they, too, speak of that day, they see it not only as the beginning of a new era, but also as a day of judgement.

So Paul assures the Corinthians that the Lord will keep them blameless 'on the day of our Lord Jesus Christ' (1 Corinthians 1:8). He points out to them that 'the day' will bring to light the true nature of every individual's life and work - and that much of it may not pass the test (3:13). He tells them to be firm in their disciplining of a wayward member, so his spirit may be saved 'on the day of the Lord' (5:5).

To the Philippians he expresses his confidence that God will complete His good work in them 'until the day of Christ Jesus' (1:6), and prays that they may be pure and blameless on that day (1:10). He urges them to live blameless lives, so that his boasting of them may not be in vain on the day of Christ (2:16).

In his second letter to Timothy, he mentions his wish that the Lord will grant mercy to Onesiphorus 'on that day' (1:18), and speaks of his hope of a crown of righteousness, which he expects the Lord to award to him and to all who love His appearing, 'on that day' (4:8).

The writer to the Hebrews urges us to be faithful in fellowship, especially in the light of the approaching of 'the day' (10:25), and Jude reminds us of the angels who sinned and who have been kept in darkness waiting for judgement 'on the great day' (Jude 6).

It is in Paul's second letter to the Thessalonians, however, that we are given the most detailed description of the events of the day of the Lord - and, in particular, of God's judgement on the wicked.

This is what he says -

> God is just: he will pay back trouble to those who trouble you and give relief to you who are troubled and to us as well. This will happen when the Lord Jesus is revealed from heaven in blazing fire with his powerful angels. He will punish those who do not know God and do not obey the gospel of our Lord Jesus. They will be punished with everlasting destruction and shut out from the presence of the Lord and from the majesty of his power on the day he comes to be glorified in his holy people and to be marvelled at among all those who have believed.
>
> (2 Thessalonians 1:6-10)

This is a very powerful passage of Scripture. In no uncertain terms it makes it very clear that the return of Christ will be an unhappy day for many people.

First of all, there will be a day of reconciliation and recompense for those who have suffered unjustly for their faith in this life. God is fair, and He will see that everything is evened out finally.

But notice the description of the parousia. Christ comes in blazing fire with powerful angels. No manger scene here! This is Christ the King taking His rightful place and reclaiming the world that is properly His. We can see once again why the nations of the world will mourn when they see Him come! The dismay, the confusion, the disbelief will be plain to see. How can it be, they will ask. How can it be that this carpenter from Nazareth Whom we dismissed so easily from our thinking as an irrelevant, impotent figure is now towering over us in indisputable and irresistible glory?!

All those who thought that they were so strong, so influential, so dominating, so self-sufficient, so independent of God or man, will find themselves cringing in terror at the fierce gaze of the Son of God.

Punishment will be meted out on two grounds only. First of all, for failure to know God, and secondly for refusal to obey the gospel of our Lord Jesus (2 Thessalonians 1:8). And here again, there will be confusion and dismay. Most people think that as long as you live a respectable life and don't do too much harm to your fellow man, God will be content.

But it is not what we know or do that counts. The important issue is *who* we know. Do we know God? We may well know about Him, but that is not the issue. Do we know Him? Personally. Genuinely. Openly.

And we must obey the good news of Jesus Christ. At first glance, this seems strange. How can you obey good news? Simply, the first act of obedience is to believe it! Many people do not. They do not accept that only through Jesus Christ and His death on the cross is their salvation.

Our tendency always is to think that by good deeds or kind actions we can save ourselves. But there is only one way of salvation, and that is through our Lord Jesus Christ. Only when we obey the good news, that if we trust Him we can be freed from sin and born from above, can we please God. All our efforts depend on our own abilities - and they always fall short. Obedience of the gospel depends on Christ's ability - and that is always sufficient.

The punishment is clear - 'everlasting destruction and shut out from the presence of the Lord and the majesty of His power'. The very exclusion from God's presence is punishment enough in itself. We do not realise that even in our sinful world, we enjoy many of God's blessings. Or, we find some kind of substitute to fill that God-shaped vacuum of which Augustine spoke.

But when there are no substitutes and there is no access to God either, the awful sense of loss must be unbearable - a kind of everlasting thirst that can never be assuaged.

There is an ancient Greek legend which in its own way suggests what being shut out from the presence of the Lord might be like. One Tantalus, who was king of Lydia, was on very intimate terms with the gods. However, he offended them, some say by sharing the food and nectar of the gods with men.

His punishment was to be chained forever in water up to his chin - but chained in such a way that every time he stooped to drink, the water level dropped just out of reach. Above his head hung succulent fruits, but they, too, were always just out of reach. Of course, the verb 'tantalise' comes from this story. Is this what it will be like to be cut off from God? Always dissatisfied, always yearning, yet never able to find satisfaction? Even the substitutes that people use will no longer be available. There will be nothing except that emptiness that only God can fill.

One additional point does need to be made about the nature of the judgement meted out. In one of His parables, Jesus laid down the principle that those who know what God wants, and refuse to do it, will be punished more severely than those who do not know the will of God, and hence fail to do it (Luke 12:47ff). So God will be scrupulously fair in His dealings with everyone. People often ask, for example, 'What about the heathen who have never heard of Christ?' The only biblical answer we can safely give to this question is that God knows all about everyone, and that no one will be condemned unfairly. In fact, Paul suggests that those who have never heard the gospel, but who live well in the light of what they do know, may be better off than those who have heard the truth, but rejected it! (Romans 2:12-16).

Peter also talks of God's judgement at the parousia of Christ. Not only will the wrath of God be displayed against those who do not know Him, but the very earth itself will be burned.

> The heavens will disappear with a roar; the elements will be destroyed by fire, and the earth and everything in it will be laid bare... That day will bring about the destruction of the heavens by fire, and the elements will melt in the heat ...
>
> (2 Peter 3:10,12)

This is a description that might well be written of a nuclear blast. But this is the hand of God wiping out everything that is stained by sin.

If it be argued that this language is metaphorical, I can only answer that in this passage it does not seem so. In fact, Peter compares this destruction by fire with the destruction of the earth in Noah's day by water. This was hardly metaphorical! The water was very real. It must be assumed that the fire of which the apostle speaks is also real.

No wonder he warns us to live godly, faithful lives, in order that we might escape the wrath of God. Without trust in God, the day of the Lord is a fearsome day indeed.

So far, we have considered what the prophets and the followers of Jesus said about the judgement of God. What about the Lord Jesus? Was He perhaps more gentle, less outspoken on such matters?

There is nothing to suggest that He was. It was He who described the nations mourning at His appearing (Matthew 24:30). It was He who also warned that judgement would come as surely as it did in the days of Noah (Matthew 24:36ff). It was He Who used phrases like 'weeping and gnashing of teeth' to describe the fate of those caught unawares by His coming (Matthew 8:12; 13:42; 22:13; 24:51; 25:30; Luke 13:28). And it was He Who warned His hearers that the day would close on them unexpectedly 'like a trap' (Luke 21:34), if they were not careful.

Moreover, there is one graphic passage in the parable of the weeds and the wheat where Jesus speaks in frightening terms -

> As the weeds are pulled up and burned in the fire, so it will be at the end of the age. The Son of Man will send out his angels, and they will weed out of his kingdom everything that causes sin and all who do evil. They will throw them into the fiery furnace, where there will be weeping and gnashing of teeth. Then the righteous will shine like the sun in the kingdom of their Father. He who has ears let him hear

> (Matthew 13:40-43)

The teaching of our Lord is very clear. He will send out angels to assemble those under penalty. Everything that has caused sin, and every evil doer will be excluded from God's presence and cast into 'the fiery furnace'. This may be literal fire, but it is more likely that the Lord is using the imagery of the parable at this point, to describe a state of eternal frustration and despair.

And notice how Jesus stresses this by His last seven words. He urges us to take careful notice of what He is saying.

65

So when we talk of the day of the Lord being a day of judgement, we are using terminology derived from both Old and New Testaments, and from both Christ and His disciples. Make no mistake, there is such a day and it will come.

Sixthly, He will come suddenly. Like lightning, He will burst on to human consciousness in a flash of unprecedented brilliance. Repeatedly, the New Testament uses the analogy of a 'thief at night' to convey this idea. If a householder knows at what time of night a thief is coming, Jesus teaches, he will keep watch and prevent his house being entered (Matthew 24:43). Peter and Paul use the same analogy (1 Thessalonians 5:2; 2 Peter 3:10).

Just as a thief comes when he is not expected, and usually when people are asleep, so will the Lord catch many people unawares when He returns.

Indeed, this is a major theme of the parables that Jesus used when talking of His coming again. In the days of Noah, people were carrying on life as usual, eating, drinking, marrying, raising families and so on. When the flood came and swept them away, they were taken completely by surprise. 'They knew nothing', said the Lord (Matthew 24:36-41).

It is interesting that Jesus does not talk about their sins in this analogy. He describes them simply as going about the normal activities of daily living. But they still were not ready! The deluge came suddenly and caught them unprepared. So, in the same way, two men will be at work, and one will be found unready and will be taken in judgement. Two women will be toiling together and one will be caught out and 'taken', because she is not prepared (Matthew 24:40).

Then Jesus uses the illustration of a servant who has been entrusted with the management of a household in his master's absence. If the man does his job faithfully, he will be rewarded when his master returns - but if he takes advantage of the situation for his own ends, he will be taken by surprise and severely punished (Matthew 24:45-51).

Finally, Jesus tells the story of the bridegroom who has gone to bring his bride from her home to his, for the wedding celebration. There are ten bridesmaids waiting for him, lamps in hand. The bridegroom is delayed and their oil supply runs low. Five have spare jars of oil; five do not. Only those whose lamps are still burning are admitted to the wedding festivities (Matthew 25:1ff).

The conclusion is simple: 'Therefore keep watch, because you do not know the day or the hour'.

It is crucial for us that we accept this statement at face value. We simply do not know when Christ will return, any more than we know when a thief will break in, or when an absent employer might turn up. He will return suddenly and unexpectedly! So we must 'keep watch'. This means living in such a way, that whenever the Lord comes, we are not caught in an embarrassing or shameful situation. It means seeing that all that is entrusted to us is being carried out wisely and well. Incidentally, it does not mean trying to calculate the date of the second coming or simply gazing into space, as it were, wistfully looking for signs in the sky, while necessary tasks around us are left undone.

Jesus Christ will return to this planet suddenly and without warning. Therefore we need to be ready.

Finally, Christ will come to establish His kingdom on the earth.

When Jesus was on trial before Pilate, He was asked whether He was a king. He answered, 'My kingdom is not of this world. If it were, my servants would fight to prevent my arrest by the Jews. But now my kingdom is from another place' (John 18:36).

At that time, the Lord refused to use anything other than love to implant the kingdom of God. The day is coming, however, when He will establish His kingdom, but this time He will do so in power.

The beautiful thing about it is that it will be a realm of peace, of justice and prosperity. The Old Testament prophets gained glimpses of this, as we saw in the last chapter. There is a particularly charming passage in Isaiah, where he begins by foretelling the earthly ministry of Jesus, but then goes on to talk of the day when the whole world will be at peace under His rule -

> The wolf will live with the lamb,
> the leopard will lie down with the goat,
> the calf and the lion and the yearling together,
> and a little child will lead them.
> The cow will feed with the bear,
> their young will lie down together,
> and the lion will eat straw like the ox.
> The infant will play near the hold of the cobra,
> and the young child will put his hand into the viper's nest.
> They will neither harm nor destroy
> on all my holy mountain,
> for the earth will be full of the knowledge of the Lord
> as the waters cover the sea.

(Isaiah 11:6-9)

In this delightful way, the prophet describes a time when the Messiah comes, in which all will be harmony and peace.

There are many similar Old Testament passages.

When we read the New Testament, we find there, also, promises of peace and prosperity to come. We have already seen how the present earth is to be destroyed by fire, but out of that will come a new earth -

and a new heaven! So Peter, having described so graphically the destruction by fire of all that we know, now goes on to say that in keeping with God's promise, we are looking forward to a new heaven and a new earth, the home of righteousness (2 Peter 3:13).

The book of Revelation draws a similar picture. In the latter chapters, the seer describes 'a new heaven and a new earth', for the first heaven and the first earth have passed away (21:1ff). Everything has been made new, and as a result there is no more pain, sorrow, tears, grief, or death.

Much of the rest of this chapter is clearly presented in symbolic language (eg the New Jerusalem's measurements). But the truth of it is unavoidable. God's intention is that both heaven and earth become a dwelling place for His people. A dwelling place in which there will be everlasting peace and contentment.

This is one of the major aims of the parousia. God has had an eternal purpose for mankind. In spite of appearances, He is neither asleep nor dead! To those who have eyes to see, in fact, He is very much alive. One day, He will fulfil all His purpose in bringing back the Edenic serenity and joy that was originally created.

It is interesting to note, in fact, that what is currently happening is virtually the original creation in reverse. In the beginning, God created the world and its flora and fauna first, and then finally he made man. In the end, it works the other way. Through the gospel, millions of men and women are becoming new creations first (2 Corinthians 5:17; Ephesians 2:10) and then ultimately the flora and fauna and the world itself will follow!

But it is all through Christ. Only in Christ Jesus is God's eternal purpose realised (Ephesians 3:1ff).

Through His first coming there is an atonement made for sin, to set right what was put wrong through the Fall. Through the second coming, there will be a cleansing of the world so that everything will be made new.

And to achieve this, Christ Himself will return personally, publicly and powerfully. He will come to gather His people to Himself, and to pronounce judgement upon the ungodly. His coming will be sudden and unexpected - but when He comes, the whole world will be given a fresh start. And the earth will be filled with the knowledge of the Lord as the waters cover the sea!

Chapter 4
When Christ Will Return

If ever there has been a popular pastime amongst Bible readers, it has been trying to predict a date for the return of Christ. The road of Christian history is littered with abandoned calculations. Strangely enough, people keep doing it!

In AD 79, for instance, a prophetess named Maximilla declared that there would be no further inspired messengers after her, but that then would come 'the consummation' (Stevenson, 1960, p.113).

The great church historian, Eusebius, recorded how an early Christian named Jude (not the one in the Bible) calculated, on the basis of Daniel's 70 weeks, that the parousia would occur in the tenth year of the emperor Severus (AD 202-203) (History, 6,5,7).

The year AD 1000 was a very popular date for the second coming, marking as it did, the end of a millennium. There was widespread expectation at that time of the end of the world (Dennet, 1960, p.90).

John Foxe, whose *Book of Martyrs* is a Christian classic, thought that the Millennium began in 324 AD, in the age of Constantine, the first Christian emperor, and concluded with the birth of John Wyclif about 1324, whom he saw as 'the morning star' heralding the establishing of Christ's kingdom, under Elizabeth, as a second Constantine! (Parker, 1965, p.17).

With its three sixes, the year AD 1666 was obviously seen as a significant date by Christians in the years leading up to it. Many believed it would mark the end of the kingdoms of this world and the beginning of the kingdom of God. 'Such dreams were

warmly cherished among the London populace ...'
(Haller, 1957, p.269f).

William Whiston (1667 - 1752), whose translation
of the writings of Josephus is still recognised as a
religious classic, thought that the so-called Lost
Tribes of Israel could be found among the Tatars and
that the millennium would begin one hundred years
later, in 1776 (LaSor in Whiston (Tr), 1969).

In 1843, William Miller, an American, calculated
that the Lord would return in 1844. Thousands of
people sold their properties and resigned their jobs in
anticipation of the great event. (Out of this came the
Seventh Day Adventist movement, who re-worked
Miller's figures.)

In 1880, H. Grattan Guinness, a cautious scholar,
who spoke disparagingly of those who glibly set dates,
nevertheless believed that the latest possible year for
the return of the Lord was around 1923. He wrote a
book of nearly 700 pages to substantiate his view
(Guinness, 1880, p.671).

In 1890, the *Christian Herald,* a journal with nearly
a quarter of a million circulation, suggested that the
year 1900 was the latest possible date for the consummation of the age.

The Irvingites expected that the Lord would return
by the death of the last of their 'apostles'. He died in
1901.

The Jehovah's Witnesses claim that the Lord
returned in 1914 and began establishing His kingdom
then.

An Australian named John Strong wrote a book, in
which he claimed that the Lord would have come back
before the end of 1978. His estimates were partly
based on calculations of the length of the passageways
and chambers of the Great Pyramid. Other pyramidologists have variously suggested 1953, 1979 and

1988 as alternatives (eg Foster, 1979, p.62).

In a very popular book published in Australia a few years ago, Stan Deyo wrote, 'There is the distinct possibility that the rapture and the tribulation may not occur until as late as 1980-81. However, I somehow doubt it...' (Deyo, 1978, p.130).

One of the most successful books ever written about the second coming is Hal Lindsey's *The Late Great Planet Earth*. He suggested that 1988 could be the date of the Lord's return (1974, p.43).

Then, of course, the year AD 2000 has been often suggested as the climax of the ages. This idea is partly based on the concept that if creation took place around 4000 BC, then the end of the twentieth century would be the completion of six 'days' of one thousand years each - with the seventh or 'sabbath' day about to dawn. (This idea was originally presented in a slightly different form in a letter written in the second century called the Epistle of Barnabas.)

These are only a few of dozens of examples that could be given of speculations and projections about the timing of the parousia. When it comes to setting dates, however, we can make only one statement with certainty - the return of Christ is nearer now than it has ever been before!

There are several dangers we face in studying this subject. *The first is ignorance of history, especially biblical history.* For instance, as we shall see, when studying passages like Jesus' Mount of Olives discourse (Matthew 24; Mark 13; Luke 21) it is necessary to know something about what was happening in Palestine at the time - and in the years immediately following that time. Jesus is clearly referring to the Roman assault on the city of Jerusalem in AD 70, in at least part of what He says. Unless we are aware of this, we cannot fully understand the

73

passage. His followers, of course, did not know about this when He first spoke to them, but many of them would still have been alive when the city was destroyed, and then they would have understood what He meant.

Similarly, in reading the prophecies of Daniel or Ezekiel, it is important to know that they were both in exile in Babylon when they wrote the books that bear their names, and hence, what they said must be read in the light of this.

The danger is that we take these passages right out of context, and, as a result, misunderstand them.

Secondly, we must beware of self-interest. I do not know of any case, for example, of people setting dates for the parousia 500 or 1000 years ahead of their own day! When dates have been calculated, they are always more or less in the individual's own era.

Obviously, this gives them much more relevance! Who is interested in the end of the age if it isn't going to happen for a thousand years?

Most evangelical believers today are premillennialists (a term we will discuss later). This is a recent development arising out of current social and political events. Fifteen hundred years ago, the popular approach was amillennialism. Two hundred years ago, postmillennialism was the prevailing view.

All of these schools of thought were substantially developed because they seemed to fit the period in question. This is not in itself wrong, of course. Naturally, we should make every attempt to make the Bible as relevant as possible to as many as possible. But we do need to be aware of the fact that where differing views are evident, we should not allow our own self-interest to lead us into extreme or uncompromising positions.

It is an interesting exercise, for example, to project ourselves back into the Middle Ages and then read the Book of Revelation. In the light of plagues like the Black Death, which wiped out one third of Europe's population; the fact that the Medieval Church owned nearly one third of all real estate; the persecution of true believers, and the ability of both secular and spiritual rulers to restrict trade and so on, it is easy to see John's visions being fulfilled then and there.

We now know, of course, that the parousia did not occur then. But it would not have been surprising if it had! The point is, that ours is not the only age when the prophetic signs seem as though they could have been fulfilled. We need to beware of seeing ourselves as so important, that all prophecy can only relate to our time. We may not be, after all, the most important generation in history!

A further danger lies in what we might call prophetic myopia - or to put it simply, a short-sighted approach to Bible prophecy. By this I mean the tendency to be so preoccupied with a study of the signs of the end of the age that we fail to plan for the future. For instance, during the 1970's there were many cases of people who were so convinced that the Lord would return before the year 2000, that they failed to consider what they should be doing in the 21st century. What plans did they have for world evangelisation, for example? What kind of training and preparation were they undergoing for the future? What kind of strategy were they implementing for church-planting in the 2000's?

By the 1980's, people began to realise that the 21st century was drawing uncomfortably near and that it was no longer possible to ignore it. So more and more people began to make plans for it. But it looked for a time as though there was a very real danger of our preoccupation with the 'signs of the times' bringing about a myopic eschatology!

DANGERS IN INTERPRETING BIBLE PROPHECY

1. IGNORANCE OF HISTORY
Both Biblical and Secular

2. SELF-INTEREST
Seeing everything only in the light of our time.

3. SHORT-SIGHTEDNESS
Failure to see the whole plan of God.

4. COMPLACENCY
It won't happen yet. (Result of too many wolf-cries?)

Fourthly, we must also beware of complacency. This is exactly the opposite problem. There is a risk of adopting an attitude of indifference towards all teaching on the return of the Lord, because of disillusionment with the frequent mistaken projections and erroneous date-setting.

This is perhaps the most serious problem of all. It is worse to be too little concerned about the parousia than too much. This is what happened after the Millerite debacle in the US in the nineteenth century. The late J. Edwin Orr wrote, 'Many people at the time lost faith in spiritual things because of the extremes of apocalyptics who followed William Miller and others …' (1965, p.99).

Aesop's fable of the boy who cried 'Wolf!' is relevant here. Those who continually make false predictions, need to be aware of the great harm they can cause by a steady erosion of credibility. On the other hand, we all need to be careful that we do not become too blase about the subject and retreat altogether from any firm convictions about the return of the Lord.

Having said all that, let's see what the Bible does teach us about the timing of the Lord's second coming. First of all, we are told in very plain terms that no-one knows! In the light of this, the pro-liferation of attempts to work it out become all the more astonishing. Here, for example, are the words of Jesus -

> No one knows about that day or hour, not even the angels in heaven, nor the Son, but only the Father. Be on guard! Be alert! You do not know when that time will come. It's like a man going away: he leaves his house and puts his servants in charge … and tells the one at the door to keep watch. Therefore keep watch because you do not know when the owner of the house will come back - whether in the evening, or at midnight, or when the rooster

crows, or at dawn. If he comes suddenly, do not let him find you sleeping. What I say to you, I say to everyone: 'Watch!'

(Mark 13:32-37)

Three times in this passage, the Lord Jesus says that we do not know the time of His return. He could hardly be more explicit. It is truly extraordinary that so many people have tried to refute this! As we have seen, time and time again, attempts have been made to prove Jesus wrong, as it were! If He tells us that we cannot know the hour of the parousia, why do we so persistently try to discover it?

Just before He ascended to heaven, the Lord re-inforced this point. 'Are you at this time going to restore the kingdom to Israel?' the Twelve asked Him. His reply was clear and plain -

It is not for you to know the times or dates which the Father has set by his own authority. But you will receive power when the Holy Spirit comes on you; and you will be my witnesses ...

(Acts 1:7f)

Once again, Jesus warns us not to become side-tracked with working out projected time frames. Rather, He says, get on with the job!

Augustine gives us similar counsel -

In vain, then, do we attempt to compute definitely the years that may remain to this world, when we may hear from the mouth of the Truth that it is not for us to know this. Yet some have said that four hundred, some five hundred, others a thousand years may be completed from the ascension of the Lord up to His final coming ... indeed they use human conjectures, and bring forward nothing certain from the authority of the canonical Scriptures.

(City of God, 18, 53)

In contrast to this, Jesus warned us that there would be some indications of His return, and that we should be able to recognise the signs.

Now learn this lesson from the fig tree: As soon as its

twigs get tender and its leaves come out, you know that summer is near. Even so, when you see these things happening, you know that it is near, right at the door.

(Mark 13:28f)

There is no contradiction between these two apparently opposite statements. In the first, Jesus makes it sky blue clear that no-one will know the time of His return. In the second, however, he warns us that we will not be totally ignorant of it either. We may not know the exact hour, but we may well have a general idea.

In the pioneering days of Australia, it sometimes took weeks for a man to make a journey to the city for trade or supplies. If he took a a bullock team, it might take months. His wife and children would know more or less when he was likely to return, but there was no way they could ever know the exact hour. It would be pointless for them to sit at the window of their bark-slab hut gazing into the bush. Or, alternatively, spending hours trying to calculate how long the journey might take, and what date he could be expected home.

There were so many variables. A flooded creek could hold him up for days. A claypan might have turned to mud and bogged his dray up to the axles. His horse might be lame. Even in the city he could be delayed waiting for a shipment of supplies. And so on.

The best his family could do was to keep things going at home as efficiently as possible and be ready, so that whenever he came, he would be welcome!

This is really as far as we need to go. To put it more simply, the reason for our Lord making the statements, he did, is to encourage us to preparation not calculation. We can never know the exact time, so we should forget about trying to work it out. Preoccupation with the calendar is especially invidious when it blinds our eyes to real human need. I have known cases, for instance, of people who have heard news of an earthquake or a major war, and have become really excited because they have seen this as a sign of the end. What they should be concerned about is the terrible suffering of the people involved, and the action needed to help them if possible.

As there may well be indications of the Lord's return, we should be prepared.

> Be dressed ready for service and keep your lamps burning, like men waiting for their master to return from a wedding banquet, so that when he comes and knocks they can immediately open the door for him ... It will be good for servants whose master finds them ready, even if he comes in the second or third watch of the night.

> (Luke 12:35ff)

This same point is made very clear in the writings of both Paul and Peter. Paul, for example, begins the fifth chapter of 1 Thessalonians like this -

> Now, brothers, about times and dates, we do not need to write to you, for you know very well that the day of the Lord will come like a thief in the night. While people are saying, 'Peace and

safety,' destruction will come on them suddenly, as labour pains on a pregnant woman, and they will not escape. But you, brothers, are not in darkness so that this day should surprise you like a thief. You are all sons of the light and sons of the day. We do not belong to the night or to the darkness. So then, let us not be like others, who are asleep, but let us be alert and self-controlled...

(1 Thessalonians 5:1-6)

The points that Paul makes here are almost the same as those made by Jesus. First of all, no-one knows the time of the parousia. Christ will come like a thief in the night. For this reason, many will be taken completely by surprise and sentenced to the wrath of God.

On the other hand, believers will not be caught out. When the Lord returns, they will be ready. But note carefully that this will not be the result of painstaking calculation of a prophetic calendar. It will be the result of a disciplined life style. Paul makes this very clear when he goes on to say -

For those who sleep, sleep at night, and those who get drunk, get drunk at night. But since we belong to the day, let us be self-controlled, putting on faith and love as a breastplate, and the hope of salvation as a helmet.

(1 Thessalonians 5:7,8)

It is by holy and upright living that we prepare for the second coming. If we are living a life pleasing to God, we shall not be caught unprepared when Jesus returns. It is clear that the major thrust of the New Testament's teaching on this subject has this aim - to encourage us to live godly lives.

Peter agrees with Paul. Since everything will be destroyed by fire, he says, what kind of people ought we to be? We ought to be living holy and godly lives as we look forward to the day of God (2 Peter 3:11).

All of this leads us to the place where we can now say that there are two major aims of biblical prophecy. One is, as we have clearly seen, *to promote holiness*. The fact that we do not know the exact hour of the Lord's appearing, makes it doubly important that we be ready when He comes.

Can you imagine what would happen, for example, if everyone did know the date? Suppose it was 15 July, 2034. What would happen on 14 July 2034? There

TWO PURPOSES OF PROPHECY

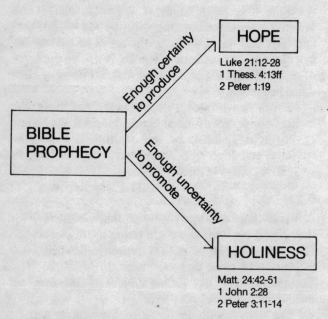

HOPE

Luke 21:12-28
1 Thess. 4:13ff
2 Peter 1:19

BIBLE PROPHECY

Enough certainty to produce

Enough uncertainty to promote

HOLINESS

Matt. 24:42-51
1 John 2:28
2 Peter 3:11-14

1 JOHN 3:3

would be a massive revival! People everywhere would suddenly become very godly. And meanwhile, they would all indulge in a flippant, hedonistic life style, doing whatever they liked, good or bad, knowing that they would have time to repent at the last minute!

Secondly, *biblical prophecy should promote hope*. We have already seen how Peter talks about believers looking forward to that day, and how Paul urges his readers to encourage each other in the light of it.

Elsewhere, Paul writes, 'We rejoice in the hope of the glory of God' (Romans 5:2). And Peter says that we have been born again into a living hope (1 Peter 1:3). On that day there will be an end to suffering and injustice. There will be universal peace and prosperity. The Lord will be king over the whole earth.

The apostle John combines both the concepts of holiness and hope when he writes, 'Everyone who has this hope in him purifies himself, just as he is pure' (1 John 3:3).

In fact, I believe that all of this points us to the intrinsic nature of Bible prophecy. Its essential function is *to draw us closer to Jesus*. The book of Revelation tells us that testimony to Christ is the essence of prophecy (Revelation 19:10). In other words, true prophecy bears faithful witness to the Lord Jesus Christ. It focuses our attention upon Him, and challenges us to be more like Him.

This helps us to understand why so many people have thought that the parousia would occur in their time. How can biblical prophecies seem to be fulfilled in so many different eras? The answer is simple. They are relevant to many different eras.

Does this mean that they are just gobbledegook? Or riddles designed to confuse us? Are they no more than the pronouncements of the oracle at the temple of Apollo in Delphi, who bathed in a sacred spring, drank the sacred water, chewed a sacred laurel leaf and then delivered utterances, intelligible or otherwise, which had to be interpreted by the priests, and then written down in safely ambiguous verse?

This would be unworthy of God. But it is true to say that prophecy is so designed that it is relevant to any age. Eventually, of course, there will be a time when there will be a final fulfilment. But meanwhile, we are faced with the fact that this could be the time! Therefore, we need to be prepared.

I believe that this divine genius impregnates all prophecy. It is so structured that it is always applicable. Consider again the possibility that there was only one possible resolution of the prophecies about the parousia, and that it was in the 21st century. For the millions of people who lived in previous centuries, large sections of the Bible would be irrelevant. It is only because we cannot say with certainty when the day of the Lord will come, that the biblical teaching about it has meaning for everyone.

Somebody once said, 'We must work as though Christ is never coming, but live as though He might come at any moment!' If you think about it, this is a helpful way to put it. Luther, for instance, is said to have commented, 'Even if I knew Christ was coming tomorrow, I would still plant a tree today' (Keeley, 1982, p.414).

It is interesting to observe that some prophecies have more than one possible application. This also gives them a continuing relevance. The best example is found in the teaching of Jesus on the Mount of Olives.

One of the most puzzling aspects of what Jesus said is the statement recorded by all three of the synoptic gospels -

I tell you the truth, this generation will certainly

not pass away until all these things have happened.

Heaven and earth will pass away, but my words will never pass away.

> (Mark 13:30,31; cf Matthew 24:34,35;
> Luke 21:32,33)

There have been many interpretations of this verse, but all of them still leave us in difficulty. I'm not sure if I have the right explanation, either, but I think that there are some helpful points that can be made. At this juncture, I would suggest that you stop reading this book and re-read the relevant passages in each of the three gospels concerned - Matthew 24, Mark 13 and Luke 21. Then it would be a good idea to keep your Bible handy for further reference as we go along.

* * * * *

The occasion for Jesus' Mount of Olives discourse was a comment by the disciples about the grandeur of Herod's temple. It was truly a magnificent structure. At this time, its construction had been in progress nearly 50 years, and it was still not completed. Its cream-coloured stones were covered with gold, and shone so brightly in the sunlight that people found it hard to look at (Josephus, *Wars*, 5, 5).

Even today, the few huge stones that remain in the area are awe-inspiring for their great size and weight. 'Look, Teacher!' said the disciples. 'What massive stones! What magnificent buildings!' (Mark 13:1).

Jesus, however, was not so impressed. 'Do you see all these great buildings?' he asked. 'Not one stone here will be left on another; every one will be thrown down' (Mark 13: 2).

This was a daring statement to make, as some of the

great building stones concerned were, according to Josephus, nearly 70 feet long and nine feet wide (Wars, 5, 5). The temple itself was one of the marvels of the ancient world.

When we read the gospels, we usually tend to think that Matthew was the first to have been written, because of the order in which the books are arranged. It is more than likely, however, that Mark was written first, although some scholars have recently opted for Luke. So let's look at the various records of this incident in reverse order, that is, Luke, Mark, Matthew.

Acording to Luke, when Jesus prophesied the destruction of the temple, the disciples asked him this question -

> Teacher, when will these things happen? And what will be the sign that they are about to take place?
>
> (21:7)

It is interesting that there is no mention here of anything about the parousia or the end of the age. They only wanted to know about the temple.

Mark's version is similar.

When we come to Matthew, however, we find that he records the Twelve as asking more than this -

> Tell us, when will this happen, and what will be the sign of your coming and of the end of the age?
>
> (24:3)

Most times, when we read Jesus' answers, we apply them only to the second two parts of this inquiry. But it is important to realise that only one gospel records the questions about the return of the Lord. All three, however, record the disciples as asking the question, 'When will the temple be destroyed?'

So we should look for answers to this question first. When we read Luke, for example, he makes the following points -
* There will be false Christs
* There will be wars and revolutions
* There will be earthquakes, famines and pestilences
* There will be fearful events and great heavenly signs
* The disciples will be persecuted
* Families will betray their own members
* There will be universal hatred of Christ's followers
* Jerusalem will be surrounded by armies
* There will be great distress
* Jewish people will be killed or enslaved to all nations
* Jerusalem will be trampled on by Gentiles

Now all of this actually refers to the fall of Jerusalem and the destruction of the temple!

When we read Mark, we find basically the same details, except for a specific reference that he makes to 'the abomination that causes desolation standing where it does not belong' (13:14), which refers to the Roman eagle being mounted in the temple.

Matthew also follows basically the same pattern, except that he also adds one or two extra points.
* False prophets will emerge with signs and wonders
* The love of most will grow cold
* The gospel will be preached to the whole world
* There will be great distress, unequaled from the beginning of the world.

Again, all of this refers to the destruction of Jerusalem. Now most of us find this hard to accept, because expressions like 'the whole world' and 'unequaled distress' and 'great signs from heaven' seem to imply universal, not local, events. But remember how Jesus said that 'this generation' would not pass away until all these things were fulfilled? Did He mean what He said? Surely He did. Therefore, He must have been talking of events from His time.

Some have argued that He was was referring to the generation that would be alive at the end of the age. If this is so, He is using the term quite differently from the way He usually did. Without exception, when Christ spoke of 'this generation' he was referring to people of His own time (eg Matthew 11:16; 12:41,42, 45; Mark 8:12,38; Luke 7:31; 11:29,30-32,50,51; 17:25). To be consistent, we must take it in this way.

Others have suggested that it means 'this race' - that is, the Jews. Again, however, this would be a most unusual word usage.

Whether we like it or not, we are forced to the conclusion that the generation Christ spoke of was His own.

So how can all the things He prophesied be true of that time? When we look at history, we can see that within forty years (which is the usually accepted time-span of a generation in the Bible) they all came to pass.

Both from the Bible and from the writings of Josephus, a Jewish historian, we find plenty of evidence for this. Within a few short years, false prophets and false Christs were evident - Simon Magus is an obvious example (Acts 8:9-13). Josephus also describes the activities of false prophets in his day, who brought ill-founded hope to a perishing city (*Wars*, 6,5).

Similarly, there were wars and revolutions - twice, the Jews rebelled against the Romans, for example (in 66 AD and 132 AD).

Christians were persecuted almost immediately after the birth of the Church. The apostles were imprisoned (Acts 4:3ff; 5:17ff). Stephen was martyred (Acts 7:57ff) and believers scattered (Acts 8:1ff).

There were even unusual signs in the heavens. Josephus describes a star resembling a sword which stood over Jerusalem and a comet that continued for a year. He also tells of an unnatural light that shone around the temple for half an hour or so (*Wars*, 6,5).

Jerusalem was surrounded by armies and eventually overrun as the Romans, under Titus, destroyed the city, causing famine and pestilence. And in some ways, this was an unequaled time of distress.

Josephus, for instance, says -

> I shall therefore speak my mind here at once briefly - That neither did any other city ever suffer such miseries, nor did any age ever breeed a generation more fruitful in wickedness than this was from the beginning of the world. (*Wars*, 5,10)

This is almost how Jesus depicted what would happen.

Josephus gives many more graphic details of the siege. It was in the year 70 AD that the armies of Vespasian, and then of Titus, his son, besieged Jerusalem. According to Josephus, Titus was benevolent and merciful, and did all he could to encourage the city's inhabitants to surrender peacefully, to save both themselves and their city. Those who did subject themselves to his clemency were usually allowed to go their way. Titus also tried to avoid destroying the temple.

However, there was sedition and division among the Jews, with rival groups causing more slaughter and destruction than the Romans. At times they combined forces, at other times they attacked each other.

Eventually the city began to suffer through famine. Titus' patience also began to run out. Some who fled were caught and crucified in full view of the inhabitants. Many still tried to escape, however, 'esteeming death from their enemies to be a quiet departure, if compared with that by famine' (*Wars*, 5,10).

Eventually, Titus had a wall built right around Jerusalem in order to cut off all escapees. Some of those who did flee, swallowed gold coins so that they could smuggle them out with them. After a while, the Romans discovered this ruse, and some of their mercenary soldiers, in particular, made a sport out of capturing these unfortunates and ripping them open with their swords, in the hope of finding the gold. On one night, two thousand people lost their lives in this way.

Meanwhile, the unscrupulous in the city itself resorted to violence, and many innocent people were put to death by their own countrymen who were looking for wealth. The shortage of food had become so acute, that others were dying of starvation. The robbers did not discriminate -

> For they brake open those houses which were no other than graves of dead bodies, and plundered them of what they had; and carrying off the coverings of their bodies, went out laughing, and tried the points of their swords on their dead bodies; and in order to prove what mettle they were made of, they thrust some of those through that still lay alive upon the ground; but for those that entreated them ... and their sword to despatch them, they were too proud to grant their requests, and left them to be consumed by famine ...(*Wars*, 5,12)

Josephus goes on to say how burial ultimately became impossible, and the corpses were simply tossed over the wall, where Titus saw the valleys 'full of dead bodies and the thick putrefaction running about them, and gave a groan; and spreading out his hands to heaven, called to God to witness that this was not his doing; but such was the sad case of the city itself' (*Wars*, 5,12).

Eventually, people resorted to searching the sewers for food. Some even ate cattle dung, so desperate were they. Others gnawed leather from belts and shoes; some gathered up old fibres.

Josephus goes on to record one horrible case, in which a desperate mother killed, cooked and ate her own little baby. To her, this was more merciful than letting him live to die a slow, agonising death. Even murderous robbers, hunting for food, were appalled at what she did (*Wars*, 6,3).

Finally, day by day, the Romans overtook the city and ultimately burned the temple. They threw its stones to the ground, as Jesus said would happen. They trod foot in the holy place, again as Jesus said. The bodies lay so thick, says Josephus, that you couldn't see the ground beneath, and the blood flowed so freely, that in places it even put out the fires.

It has been calculated that in all, nearly one and a half million Jews lost their lives at this time! (*Wars*, 6, 9, note).

Josephus concludes -

> The multitude of those that therein perished exceeded all the destructions that either men or God ever brought upon the world. (*Wars*, 6, 9)

The horror of those days is clearly protrayed by Josephus. They were abominable times and truly fulfil the terms of the prophecies of Jesus. What He said did happen.

As for the gospel being preached in the whole world, this had come about by the time Jerusalem fell - at least as far as the known world was concerned. In his letter to the Colossians, for example, Paul writes, 'All over the world this gospel is bearing fruit and is growing' (Colossians 1:6). He takes this even further when he says, 'This ... gospel ... has been proclaimed to every creature under heaven' (1:23).

It is interesting to note that biblical writers sometimes spoke of the world in a general, rather than a literal sense. For example, at Pentecost, it is recorded that there were Jews present 'from every nation under heaven' (Acts 2:5), a designation that we now know to be incorrect, but which, in the terminology of the day, was quite acceptable.

Finally, literal evidence of the destruction of Herod's temple may be seen clearly today in Jerusalem. Only in recent years have some of the huge stones been uncovered that the Romans rolled into the valley beneath the Temple Mount. If you go there, you can actually touch, lean against or sit on the building blocks of which Jesus spoke. Only the retaining wall, (the famous Western Wall or 'Wailing Wall'), which was not actually part of the building, and the southern steps leading up to the temple, remain.

It was only after Jesus dealt with the fall of Jerusalem that He began to talk of the parousia. According to Luke's version, Jerusalem was to be trampled down 'until the times of the Gentiles' were fulfilled (21:24). After this, there would be signs of the Lord's return.

According to Mark, 'after' the distress of Jerusalem's collapse there would be signs of the parousia (13:24). Matthew agrees (24:29).

All the gospel writers then go on to say that the following would occur -
* the sun and moon darkened
* signs in the sun, moon and stars
* stars falling
* nations in anguish and perplexity at the roaring and tossing of the sea
* men fainting from terror and apprehension of what is coming on the world
* the heavenly bodies shaken

* the sign of the Son of Man in the sky
* the return of Christ

The specific signs of the end of the age are relatively few. Also, their exact nature is not as clear as they might be. In what ways will the sun and moon be darkened? For how long? What does it mean that heavenly bodies will be shaken? We shall only know when we see these things actually happening. Obviously, these signs mean more than just an eclipse or a meteorite shower.

In the light of the fact that Jesus said that *all* the signs would occur in that generation, at least one writer suggests that they were all fulfilled in the fall of Jerusalem, when Christ came in 'clouds of judgement' on Israel and took the kingdom from them (Chilton, 1987, pp.64-67).

Is some of this language metaphorical? For instance, why would nations be perplexed by the roaring and tossing of the sea? Could this be the sea of humanity? Time will tell. Certainly, we can see even in our own day, the restless surging of the peoples of the world as underprivileged, racially disadvantaged, politically oppressed and suffering people struggle for survival.

Earlier in this chapter, I made the point that the genius of Bible prophecy lies in the fact that it is always relevant. This has to be true of the teaching of Christ, which is the most significant of all on this subject. If it only refers to the destruction of Jerusalem, how does it apply to us? It is no more than an object lesson of fulfilled prophecy.

In fact, it does seem to be more than this. This is why the language that Jesus uses appears to be too extensive for the collapse of a small city in a tiny Middle Eastern country. While Jesus is talking specifically of the fall of Jerusalem, He is also talking of the kind of thing that will happen over and over again, in other places, during the course of human history as well.

Not only would there be distress in Jerusalem, but during the whole Christian age, there would be distress and tribulation. Not only would false pophets arise in His day, but they would continue to do so for generations to come. Similarly, there would be ongoing persecution and betrayal and warfare and revolution and so on.

At first glance, this might appear like playing with words. But it is, in fact, a feature of biblical prophecy. Let's take a couple of Old Testament examples. The prophet Hosea once wrote, 'Out of Egypt I called my son' (Hosea 11:1). This is a reference to the exodus, when the nation of Israel (God's 'son') was rescued from the slavery of the pharoahs. Matthew, however, takes this passage and claims that it was a prophecy fulfilled when Mary and Joseph brought Jesus back from Egypt to Nazareth, after the death of Herod (Matthew 2:15).

Likewise, Isaiah prophesied that a young woman, who was at the time a virgin, would give birth to a son and that before this son was old enough to know right from wrong, the land of Judah would be liberated from the threat of the two enemy kings of Aram and Israel (Isaiah 7:14-16). The indication is that this was Isaiah's own son (8:3,4). But again, Matthew takes this prophecy and applies it to the birth of Jesus whose mother was not only a virgin at the time of the prophecy, but was still a virgin at the time of the birth!

And so we could go on. There are many Old Testament prophecies which have multiple fulfilments. This is not a sneaky trick on God's part. He is not trying to give us double-dealing promises like the witches in Macbeth, whose predictions also had a secondary meaning, but a meaning quite different from the apparent one. In biblical prophecies, even where there is a secondary or further application, it is still essentially of the same nature. In every case the meaning is true and direct. What God is doing is to encourage several groups of people, in different ages, with the same words!

The apostle Peter indicates that many prophets were themselves aware of the fact that their prophecies seemed to contain implications beyond their own time.

> Concerning this salvation, the prophets, who spoke of the grace that was to come to you, searched intently and with the greatest care, trying to find out the time and circumstances to which the Spirit of Christ in them was pointing when he predicted the sufferings of Christ and the glories that would follow. It was revealed to them that they were not serving themselves but you, when they spoke of the things that have now been told you by those who have preached the gospel to you by the Holy Spirit sent from heaven.

(1 Peter 1:10-12)

We could say that this is something like a man about to climb a mountain. He sees the peak ahead and thinks that he has almost reached the top. When he finally attains this height, however, he finds that there is a higher peak still ahead, which he could not see before. So a prophet sees an immediate application for his word, but knows only dimly of the long-term subsequent fulfilments.

For many prophecies in the Bible there is both a primary and a secondary application - and then multiple personal applications, as believers over the ages apply the truths concerned to themselves.

So what Jesus says about the fall of Jerusalem, may equally have a further fulfilment in later times. This could still apply again to Jerusalem - as indeed many people believe it will (eg Lindsey, 1974, p. 42ff). Or, it could apply to the Church, the new, spiritual Jerusalem. Certainly, it can encourage any believer of any age who finds himself in a similar situation.

INTERPRETING BIBLE PROPHECY. . . 1

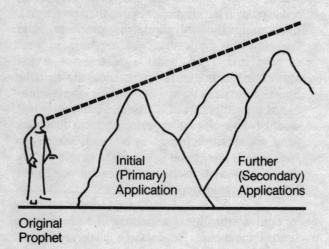

Initial
(Primary)
Application

Further
(Secondary)
Applications

Original
Prophet

The original prophet cannot see subsequent fulfilments because he is too close to the initial one. But he knows there is something beyond and yearns to see it.

Numbers 12:6-8
1 Peter 1:10-12
1 Cor 9:8-12; 10:11-13

For example, when Jesus spoke of His followers being hauled before magistrates, He promised them that the Holy Spirit would help them to know what to say (Mark 13:11; Luke 21:14f). The same promise can be claimed by any believers in similar situations. When He assured them that, in spite of all that anyone could do, not a hair of their heads would perish, and that those days would be shortened for the sake of the elect (Luke 21:18; Matthew 24:22), He was making promises that anyone could claim at any time if needed.

Bible prophecy, then, is always relevant to every situation.

This is precisely why so many people have been convinced that the parousia was about to occur in their day! They could well have been right. It might have been possible. As it happens, it was not. But one day, of course, the Lord will return, and he will come in accordance with the signs that He talked about.

What we need to stress, however, is that the major thrust of eschatalogical teaching in the Bible is *hope* and *holiness*.

We are given divine promises of the Lord's return to encourage us. We are assured that in all of the times of trouble that may eventuate, the Lord is in control, and that He is coming back one day to take over. We are also encouraged to live holy and godly lives so that we are ready when He comes.

What we are not told to do is to spend out time trying to calculate the date or the hour of His return. This information is classified top secret. It is for His eyes only.

Chapter 5
For Whom Christ Will Return

Our vision of the return of Christ affects everything crucial in our lives. It determines our attitude to the future. It influences the kind of work we commit ourselves to, the place where we choose to live, and the kind of friendships we develop.

It affects the choice of our church, our theology and our ministry. Some pervading idea of the coming of Christ lies behind our decisions in marriage, in having children, in our attitude to death. It is a major factor on how we seek to prepare ourselves and our families to face what lies ahead. It affects our finances. It affects our commitment. It deeply affects our desire to be prepared to meet God.

> 'The primitive church thought more about the Second Coming of Jesus Christ than about death or heaven. They were not looking for a cleft in the ground called a grave, but a cleavage in the sky called Glory. They were not watching for the "undertaker" but the "Uppertaker".'
>
> (Alexander MacLaren).

Kenneth Scott Latourette (former President of the American Historical Society) replied to a questioner: 'I believe that our Lord may return at any time and bring this present stage of history to an end. That may well be between now and the year A.D. 2000'.

The Church is to be a people looking forward to

Jesus' return. We see now a hunger to restage again ancient prophetic history: our world once more both needs and awaits a Messiah. The battle for our time is not to believe in a Christ; but to believe and commit ourselves to the rightful One.

> 'The Old Testament tells us what Christ is, the New Testament tells us *Who* He is, and in such a way that … he alone knows Jesus who recognizes Him as the Christ and he alone knows who "the Christ" is who knows that He is Jesus'
>
> (Erich Sauer)

The godly prophet Daniel living long ago in Babylon, a techno-psychic culture much like ours today, was given a glimpse of this rightful coming Ruler in a vision so staggering that spiritual as he was, it left him days and nights without sleep:

> In my vision at night I looked, and there before me was one like a Son of Man, coming with the clouds of heaven. He approached the Ancient of Days and was led into his presence. He was given authority, glory and sovereign power; all peoples, nations and men of every language worshipped him. His dominion is an everlasting dominion that will not pass away, and his kingdom is one that will never be destroyed … but the saints of the Most High will receive the kingdom and will possess it - yes, for ever and ever.
>
> (Daniel 7:13, 14, 18)

All people. Nations. Languages. Who are these 'saints of the most high?' Just exactly *for whom* will Jesus come? The prophecies of His first coming were fulfilled with awesome accuracy and detail, despite astronomical odds for accident and coincidence; and yet for every prophecy of His first coming there are around *seven* of His second! Scripture not only makes plain that Jesus *will* come, it also tells us in detail *for whom* He is coming.

It is one thing to know and be convinced He *is* coming; it is quite another to be prepared and ready. Will you be ready for that Ultimate Encounter? How do you know? Here is the Bible record on whom He will come for when He returns:

Dead Men Twice-Born

1. *Jesus is coming for those who have given up their lives to Him,* losing themselves in His service and for His sake.

> If anyone would come after me, he must deny himself and take up his cross and follow me. For whoever wants to save his life will lose it, but whoever loses his life for me will find it ... For the Son of Man is going to come in his Father's glory with his angels, and then he will reward each person according to what he has done.

> (Matthew 16:24-27)

Jesus is coming first of all for those who *belong* to Him. The Bible makes it clear that to be a true child of God we must renounce all self-effort and self-centred living, and wholly abandon ourselves to the sacrifice and righteousness of Christ. Selfishness is incompatible with true Christianity. The good news of salvation changes a person wholly and totally and makes him His devoted servant and lover forever:

> Our gospel came to you not simply with words but also with power, with the Holy Spirit and with deep conviction. You know how we lived among you for your sake. You became imitators of us and

of the Lord; in spite of severe suffering you welcomed the message with joy given by the Holy Spirit ... The Lord's message rang out from you ... your faith in God has become known everywhere ... how you turned to God from idols to serve the living and true God, and to wait for his Son from heaven, whom he raised from the dead - Jesus, who rescues us from the coming wrath.

(1 Thessalonians 1:5-10)

God Reaps Where He Has Not Sown

2. *Jesus is coming for those who have been faithful in what was entrusted to them,* who have used what was given them wisely, with initiative and in faith:

A man of noble birth went into a distant country to have himself appointed king and then to return. So he called ten of his servants and gave them ten minas. 'Put this money to work,' he said, 'until I come back'.

(Luke 19:12, 13)

Here Jesus speaks of Himself as one who 'takes up' what He has not 'laid down' and 'reaping that I did not sow' (Luke 19:22) and intimates that His servants are not to be passive in their waiting. They must show enterprise and investment, to use initiative with what has been given them, (even perhaps to take calculated risks!), so when their Master returns they can return to Him even more than He left them.

God likewise gives to all His true children some gift of grace to bring Him honour:

I always thank God for you because of his grace given you in Christ Jesus. For in him you have been enriched in every way - in all your speaking

101

and in all your knowledge - because our testimony about Christ was confirmed in you. Therefore you do not lack any spiritual gift as you eagerly wait for our Lord Jesus Christ to be revealed. He will keep you strong to the end, so that you will be blameless on the day of our Lord Jesus Christ.

(1 Corinthians 1:4-8)

However, we are never to use any improved positions of power, success or wealth as a result of such enterprise with the gifts of God, to defraud, oppress or injure others; we are to live in the humility of constant awareness that the Judge of all the earth may return at any moment and call us into eternal account:

Be patient then, brothers, until the Lord's coming. See how the farmer waits for the land to yield its valuable crop and how patient he is for the autumn and spring rains. You, too, be patient and stand firm, because the Lord's coming is near. Don't grumble against each other, brothers, or you will be judged. The Judge is standing at the door!

(James 5:7-9)

Don't Play God For Others

3. *Jesus is coming for those who will take their own personal life direction from Him until death,* and neither seek to compare God's dealings with them to that of others, nor seek to know the future of others with whom He is also working:

When Peter saw John, he asked, 'Lord, what about him?' Jesus answered, 'If I want him to remain alive until I return, what is that to you? You must follow *me*'.

(John 21:21, 22)

Although we are not to seek to know God's dealings with the future of *others,* we *are* ourselves to live in a personal sense of Divine history and destiny. Scripture warns of a time like ours; what happens to a world that rejects or supresses both the Biblical and natural revelation of man's God-created origin? Ultimately it becomes cynical over its God-appointed destiny - the coming confrontation with the Ruler of the Universe:

> First of all, you must understand that in the last days scoffers will come, scoffing and following their own evil desires. They will say, 'Where is this "coming" he promised?' ... But they deliberately forget that long ago by God's word the heavens existed and the earth was formed out of water and by water. By these waters also the world of that time was deluged and destroyed. By the same word the present heavens and earth are reserved for fire, being kept for the day of judgement and destruction of ungodly men.

> But do not forget this one thing, dear friends: With the Lord a day is like a thousand years, and a thousand years are like a day. The Lord is not slow in keeping his promise, as some understand slowness. He is patient with you, not wanting anyone to perish, but everyone to come to repentance.

> (2 Peter 3:3-9)

Believe It - Not!

4. *Jesus is coming for those freed from personal religious fantasy and the dangers of sophisticated demonic deception:*

> At that time, if anyone says to you, 'Look, here is the Christ!' or, 'There he is!' do not believe it. For

103

false Christs and false prophets will appear and perform great signs and miracles to deceive even the elect - if that were possible. See, I have told you ahead of time.

So if anyone tells you, 'There he is, out in the desert,' do not go out; or, 'Here he is, in the inner rooms,' do not believe it. For as the lightning that comes from the east is visible even in the west, so will be the coming of the Son of Man.

(Matthew 24:23-27)

Jesus is coming for those whose faith is rooted in the objective *facts* of history and Scripture. He is coming for those who are Christians because they have given their lives to Him Who is both reality and truth:

We did not follow cleverly invented stories when we told you about the power and coming of our Lord Jesus Christ, but we were eyewitnesses of his majesty. For he received honour and glory from God the Father when the voice came to him from the Majestic Glory, saying, 'This is my Son, whom I love; with him I am well pleased.' We ourselves heard this voice that came from heaven when we were with him on the sacred mountain. And we have the word of the prophets made more certain, and you will do well to pay attention to it, as a light shining in a dark place, until the day dawns and the morning star rises in your hearts.

(2 Peter 1:16-19)

Not Ashamed To Be Called Their God

5. *Jesus is coming for those not bound by fear or shame to commit themselves both to Him and His Word,* nor to confess Him and His truth in an immoral, scoffing world:

If anyone is ashamed of me and my words in this adulterous and sinful generation, the Son of Man will be ashamed of him when he comes in his Father's glory with the holy angels.

(Mark 8:38)

Our witness must be kind and gentle, not argumentative and critical; we are called to tell the truth, not defend it, to proclaim it, not persecute with it.

Do everything without complaining or arguing, so that you may become blameless and pure, children of God without fault in a crooked and depraved generation, in which you shine like stars in the universe as you hold out the word of life - in order that I may boast on the Day of Christ that I did not run or labour for nothing.

(Philippians 2:14-16)

We are to live lives that show we really are people who love all nations, because we belong to the greatest one; who belong to all peoples because we belong to another world; and in so doing we will not only not be ashamed to own the real God as ours but neither will He be ashamed to own us as His.

(Hebrews 11:16)

And now, little children, continue in him, so that when he appears we may be confident and unashamed before him at his coming.

(1 John 2:28)

Only Forty More Shopping Days Till The End Of The World (Californian Bumper Sticker)

6. *Jesus will come for those careful to stay unsnared*

105

by the universal lures of materialism and excess, in which the grind of empty daily life feels like the giddy headache of a sick drunkard:

> Be careful, or your hearts will be weighed down with dissipation, drunkenness and the anxieties of life, and that day will close on you unexpectedly like a trap. For it will come upon all those who live on the face of the whole earth. Be always on the watch, and pray that you may be able to escape all that is about to happen, and that you may be able to stand before the Son of Man.
>
> (Luke 21:34-36)

Paul lists *five sins* that caused the loss of an entire generation in the wilderness, who never made it to their final destination, who missed out completely on the promised land given by God. God in full integrity provided a new world for them but they perished instead in their presumption.

He tells us this record applies as a special warning to those who live in the time of the end of the world:

> These things (lust, idolatry, fornication, tempting Christ and irritable grumbling) happened to them as examples and were written down as warnings for us, on whom the fulfilment of the ages has come. So if you think you are standing firm, be careful that you don't fall!
>
> (1 Corinthians 10:1-12)

Knowledge that we are citizens of another world, that we are 'not home yet' will remind us not only that we are special in the eyes of God, but set apart while we live in this world:

> For the grace of God that brings salvation has appeared to all men. It teaches us to say 'No' to ungodliness and worldly passions, and to live self-

106

controlled, upright and godly lives in this present age, while we wait for the blessed hope - the glorious appearing of our great God and Saviour, Jesus Christ, who gave himself for us to redeem us from all wickedness and to purify for himself a people that are his very own, eager to do what is good.

(Titus 2:11-14)

Let your gentleness be evident to all. The Lord is near.

(Philippians 4:5)

Coming Ready Or Not

7. *Jesus is coming for those who are alert, watching and prayerfully ready at any time for the wholly unexpected:*

No one knows about that day or hour, not even the angels in heaven or the Son, but only the Father ... Therefore keep watch, because you do not know on what day your Lord will come. But understand this: If the owner of the house had known at what time of the night the thief was coming, he would have kept watch and would not have let his house be broken into. So you also must be ready, because the Son of Man will come at an hour when you do not expect him.

(Matthew 24:36, 42, 43)

It is not for you to know the times or the dates the Father has set by his own authority.

(Acts 1:7)

If not even *the Son* knew the day of His return and it

was to be left in the sole hands of the Father, what sense does it make for *us* to try to predict it?

Be on guard! Be alert! You do not know when that time will come. It's like a man going away: He leaves his house in charge of his servants each with his assigned task, and tells the one at the door to keep watch.

Therefore, keep watch because you do not know when the owner of the house will come back - whether in the evening, or at midnight, or when the cock crows, or at dawn. If he comes suddenly, do not let him find you sleeping. What I say to you, I say to everyone: 'Watch!'

(Mark 13:33-36)

Here Comes The Judge!

8. *Jesus is coming for those who by grieving prayer, aggressive faith, and patient intercession, cry out for and expect His divine intervention and justice in human affairs:*

So do not throw away your confidence; it will be richly rewarded. You need to persevere so that when you have done the will of God, you will receive what he has promised. For in just a little while, 'He who is coming will come and will not delay. But my righteous one will live by faith. And if he shrinks back, I will not be pleased with him'.

(Hebrews 10:35-38)

Jesus also spoke of the need for *perseverance in prayer* (in the parable of the unjust judge) but hinted in Luke 18 that it might be a rare commodity when He returned:

However, when the Son of Man comes, will he find faith on the earth?

(Luke 18:8)

Because the return of Christ is the *ultimate expression of true justice,* it is something every true Christian should look foward to. On that day all men will know the *real* reason everything was done: on that day the motive behind every act will be revealed, and the true heart of all decisions held up for all the world to see. It is terror to the sinner and joy to the saint:

All this is evidence that God's judgement is right, and as a result you will be counted worthy of the kingdom of God, for which you are suffering. God is just: He will pay back double to those who trouble you and give relief to you who are troubled, and to us as well. This will happen when the Lord Jesus is revealed from heaven in blazing fire with his powerful angels. He will punish those who do not know God and do not obey the gospel of our Lord Jesus. They will be punished with everlasting destruction and shut out from the presence of the Lord and from the majesty of his power on the day he comes to be glorified in his holy people and to be marvelled at among all those who have believed ...

(2 Thessalonians 1:6-10)

The Ultimate Terror

9. *Jesus is coming for those who have the fear of the Lord.* The true God is at once the most lovely and scary Person in the Universe; to fear Him now, to give Him the awesome reverence due Him, is to be better ready for the day when He is revealed in majesty as the rightful Ruler of the Universe. The return of Christ is not only the climax of human history; it is rightfully the most *terrifying* event of all time:

For the Son of Man in his day will be like the light-

ning which flashes and lights up the sky, from one
end to the other.

(Luke 17:24)

Clouds and thick darkness surround him,
Righteousness and justice are the foundation of his
throne.
Fire goes before him and consumes his foes on
every side.
His lightning lights up the world;
The earth sees and trembles.
The mountains melt like wax before the Lord,
Before the Lord of all the earth.
The heavens proclaim His righteousness,
And all the peoples see His glory.

(Psalm 97:2-6)

Isaiah pleaded with God to rend the heavens and
come down with such power, that the mountains would
tremble before him (Isaiah 64:1ff). As a fire sets water
boiling, so, said Isaiah, the nations would tremble
before God. Clearly, Isaiah saw the awesomeness of
his God:
Since ancient times no one has heard,
no ear has perceived,
no eye has seen any God besides you,
who acts on behalf of those who wait for him

(Isaiah 64:4)

This is what the Lord Almighty says: 'In a little
while I will once more shake the heavens and the
earth, the sea and the dry land. I will shake all
nations, and the desired of all nations will come,
and I will fill this house with glory,' says the Lord
Almighty.

(Haggai 2:6-7)

10. *Jesus will return for those who do not forget Him:*
who hold in continual remembrance His atoning death
for our sins on the cross, celebrate His victorious
resurrection and encourage His covenant love among
believers.

It is for this reason we are exhorted to remember the
New Covenant He made with us by His vicarious
suffering, and the offering of His body and blood to
redeem us:

> For whenever you eat this bread and drink this
> cup, you proclaim the Lord's death until he
> comes'.

(1 Corinthians 11:26)

God has been hurt by the sin of men, but at great cost
to Himself has made a way back to His heart through
His Son:

> Christ would have had to suffer since the creation
> of the world. But now he has appeared once for all
> at end of the world to do away with sin by the
> sacrifice of himself. Just as man is destined to die
> once, and after that to face judgement, so Christ
> was sacrificed once to take away the sins of many
> people; and he will appear a second time, not to
> bear sin, but to bring salvation to those who are
> waiting for him.

(Hebrews 9:26-28)

To live in this conscious freedom means to live loose
to the world; *in* it but not *of* it; to show by our love for
each other that the Triune God is real.

Since, then, you have been raised with Christ, set
your hearts on things above, where Christ is seated at

the right hand of God. Set your minds on things above, not on earthly things. For you died, and your life is now hidden with Christ in God. When Christ, who is your life, appears, then you also will appear with him in glory ... Therefore, as God's chosen people, holy and dearly loved, clothe yourselves with compassion, kindness, humility, gentleness and patience. Bear with one another and forgive whatever grievances you may have against one another. Forgive as the Lord forgave you. And over all these virtues put on love, which binds them all together in perfect unity. Let the peace of Christ rule in your hearts, since as members of one body you were called to peace. And be thankful.

(Colossians 3:1-4, 12-15)

It is the *love* Christians show to each other that is the most powerful testimony of Christ's reality; that is why we are to meet often together in fellowship:

Let us hold unswervingly to the hope we profess, for he who promised is faithful. And let us consider how we may spur one another on to love and good deeds. Let us not give up meeting together, as some are in the habit of doing, but let us encourage one another - and all the more as you see the Day approaching.

(Hebrews 10:24-25)

What is the great joy of the true Christian? To see others meet the Lord. Every new-born Christian is a foretaste of heaven.

For what is our hope, our joy, or the crown in which we will glory in the presence of our Lord Jesus when he comes? Is it not you? Indeed, you are our glory and joy.

(1 Thessalonaians 2:19)

11. *Jesus is coming for those (like God Himself) who are happy living a holy and right life* and who in so doing, know something of both the works and the ways of God in His people:

> Now this is our boast: Our conscience testifies that we have conducted ourselves in the world, and especially in our relations with you, in the holiness and sincerity that are from God ... as you have understood us in part, you will come to understand fully that you can boast of us just as we will boast of you in the day of the Lord Jesus.
>
> (2 Corinthians 1:12, 14)

If God has begun a true work in your life, He will complete it. He is the Alpha and Omega, the Originator and Completer, simultaneously our Source and our Goal:

> Being confident of this, that he who began a good work in you will carry it on to completion until the day of Christ Jesus ... so that you may be able to discern what is best and may be pure and blameless until the day of Christ, filled with the fruit of righteousness that comes through Jesus Christ - to the glory and praise of God.
>
> (Philippians 1:6, 10-11)

> May the Lord make your love increase and overflow for each other and for everyone else, just as ours does for you. May he strengthen your hearts so that you will be blameless and holy in the presence of our God and Father when our Lord Jesus comes with all his holy ones.
>
> (1 Thessalonians 3:12-13)

God our Father is going to have a beautiful Bride ready for the wedding of His Son: 'May God himself, the God of peace, sanctify you through and through. May your whole spirit, soul and body be kept blameless at the coming of our Lord Jesus Christ.

(1 Thessalonians 5:23).

Let us rejoice and be glad
and give him glory!
For the wedding of the Lamb has come,
and his bride has made herself ready
(Revelation 19:7)

We Are Not The Only Ones Anticipating The Day

12. *Jesus is coming for those who love Him, and we are to look forward to His return with great joy and gladness.* But Jesus Himself is also looking forward to this time, when He and His beautiful Bride begin the eternal honeymoon that lies before us:

For the joy set before him, he endured the cross, scorning its shame, and sat down at the right hand of the throne of God.

(Hebrews 12:2)

John the Baptist said it on the banks of Jordan in anticipation of that great Wedding day: 'You yourselves can testify that I said, ''I am not the Christ but am sent ahead of him.'' The bride belongs to the bridegroom. The friend who attends the bridegroom waits and listens for him, and is full of joy when he hears the bridegroom's voice (John 3:28, 29).

A Divine Voice is in the air again, whispering to His Bride that her lovely and great King is coming:

My beloved spoke and said to me, 'Arise my

darling, my beautiful one, and come with me'.

(Song of Solomon 2:10)

Jesus is coming, and His is a Coming of both an unimaginable Love and an overwhelming Majesty. Before that day we must know something of the glory of His Presence, with a real relationship to Him as our Lord and Saviour. No man or woman in the world can look forward to his coming without this.

If we don't love Him now, that great day will be the most awful day of our lives. Saul, that violent young intellectual, who first met Him on the road to Damascus, understood just how wonderful and terrible such a first shielded encounter could be. It blinded him, humbled him, gave him a new name and made him a brand-new man. It changed his world for-ever, and through him and thousands of others in turn, that initial Divine encounter went on to affect the world to come.

'Now' he said, 'there is in store for me a crown of righteousness, which the Lord, the righteous Judge, will award me on that day - and not only to me, but also to all who have longed for his appearing' (2 Timothy 4:8).

As C.S. Lewis so powerfully put it:

'God is going to invade all right; but what is the good of saying you are on His side then when you see the whole natural universe melting away like a dream and something else - something it never entered your head to conceive - comes crashing in; something so beautiful to some of us and so terrible to others that none of us will have any choice left?

For this time it will be God without disguise; something so overwhelming that it will strike either irresistible love or irresistible horror into

115

every creature. It will be too late then to choose your side. There is no use saying you choose to lie down when it has become impossible to stand up. That will not be the time for choosing; it will be the time when we discover which side we really have chosen whether we realized it before or not. Now, today, this moment is our chance to choose the right side. God is holding back to give us that chance. It will not last forever. We must take it or leave it.'

(Mere Christianity, 1977, p.66)

Jesus is coming for His Bride. Only His true Bride and the friends of the Bridegroom can look forward to the Great Event.

Are you ready?

PART TWO

Questions and Answers

PART TWO

Questions and Answers

1. Why are there so many different opinions about the return of Christ?

After reading some of the books on the subject, it would be easy to suggest that there are as many opinions as there are people! However, in reality, there are about four major schools of thought about eschatology (ie a study of the end of the age, from *eschatos* = 'last' and *logos* = 'word, reason, study'). These views usually represent variant approaches to the Book of Revelation in particular.

The first is the *praeterist* view. This is the belief that the prophecies of the Book of Revelation have mainly been fulfilled already. It comes from the Latin verb *praeterire* which means 'to pass by' or 'to go by'. Praeterism is the belief that the events described in Revelation have already 'gone by'.

Hence, for the praeterist, the seven kings of Revelation 17 were seven Roman emperors, the number 666 refers to Nero, the harlot of chapter 17 is Rome who, through her fierce persecution of Christians was 'drunk with the blood of the saints' (17:6), and so on.

Naturally, the letters to the seven churches apply literally to those actual churches, and the various plagues and judgements were fulfilled in the days of the Early Church.

This view tends to be favoured by scholars in the more traditional churches.

The positive value of the praeterist view is that it has a sound starting point - namely, the seer's own day. It is a wise principle of biblical interpretation always to begin with the contemporary situation of the writer concerned and to work from there. This applies to the Old Testament prophets in particular, but also to the

PRAETERIST SCHOOL OF INTERPRETATION

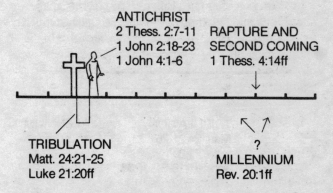

ANTICHRIST
2 Thess. 2:7-11
1 John 2:18-23   RAPTURE AND
1 John 4:1-6   SECOND COMING
                    1 Thess. 4:14ff

TRIBULATION   ?
Matt. 24:21-25   MILLENNIUM
Luke 21:20ff   Rev. 20:1ff

New Testament writers as well, whether their writings be historical or apostolic or prophetic.

For instance, it is easier to understand Paul's letters if we know something of the background of the people to whom he wrote, together with his reasons for writing.

It is certainly true of the book of Revelation, that some knowledge of the perspective from which John wrote is helpful. It is clear that much of the book does refer to contemporary people and events.

On the other hand, if, like the praeterist, we say that basically all of the book is to be understood in this way, we make it largely irrelevant to readers of all later generations. This is a major weakness with praeterism. As we have seen already, the essence of prophecy is that it is always relevant.

Another approach is the *historicist*. This school of

HISTORICIST SCHOOL
OF INTERPRETATION

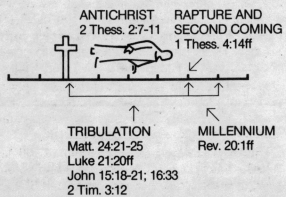

ANTICHRIST
2 Thess. 2:7-11

RAPTURE AND
SECOND COMING
1 Thess. 4:14ff

TRIBULATION
Matt. 24:21-25
Luke 21:20ff
John 15:18-21; 16:33
2 Tim. 3:12

MILLENNIUM
Rev. 20:1ff

thought suggests that Revelation presents in prophetic form an overview of human history from Christ's first coming to His second.

So, like the praeterist, the historicist begins in the first century, with the Roman Empire, but then goes on from there to the present day. The seven churches of chapters two and three, for example, are seen as symbolising seven ages of the Church from the first century to the return of Christ (eg Foster, 1977). The seven trumpets (chapters 7-9), for instance, are seen as representing the Goths, the Vandals, the Huns, the Heruli, the Arabs, the Turks and the Communists - a series which stretches from AD 400 to AD 1917. The Beast (or the Antichrist) is seen, not as an individual, but usually as the institution of the papacy. The 'little book' of chapter 10 is the Bible, printed and distributed by the Reformers.

Fundamental to the historicist view is the concept that each 'day' mentioned by the seer represents a year (Guinness, 1880, p.295ff). The key to this is seen in Ezekiel 4:6 where God tells Ezekiel that He has assigned him 'a day for each year'. Hence, 1260 days means 1260 years and so on. Guinness compares this to a cartographer who draws a map to a scale where, for example, one inch represents 100 miles (1880, p.299). With the correct scale, we can then correctly interpret all the time measurements in the prophetic Scriptures.

Obviously, there is a huge difference between a period of 1260 days and one of 1260 years, for example! And equally obviously, the resultant understanding of Scripture will be very different.

Similarly, in Revelation, each group of 360 days is called a 'time' (12:6,14). If each day in turn becomes a year, then each 'time', in fact, represents 360 years. (This is all based on a lunar year, of course.) So the seven 'times' mentioned in Leviticus 26:28 as a period of punishment for Israel are seen as a total period of 2,520 years (eg Guinness, 1880, pp. 344ff).

Depending on when you begin this period, it usually finishes somewhere around 1940. The only problem with this particular aspect of historicism is that the actual word 'time' does not occur at all in the original Hebrew text of Leviticus! The meaning is probably 'sevenfold', that is a reference to intensity rather than duration.

The historicist view has some appealing features. It makes the Revelation, at least in part, relevant for every era. It commences its interpretation in the first century, which is, as I have suggested, the essential starting point for any such study. It avoids some of the more fanciful imaginings of those who squeeze all the prophecies into the last few years of time.

On the other hand, all historicists seem to work out a scheme that finishes more or less in their own day, and so their interpretations have been revised and updated at regular intervals. This has resulted in a significant divergence of ideas about the correct meaning of many prophecies - and this very divergence means that, at the most, only one of them can be right!

Further, it seems unlikely to me that God would inspire a form of prophecy that depends so heavily on historical knowledge for its understanding. If this were the case, then the book would be basically meaningless to first century Christians, who could not possibly have the requisite historical knowledge, and to people of any subsequent century who were not students of history.

The historicist view became popular during the Reformation and was held in one form or another by some of the Reformers. It is not as widely taught today as the other views.

The third view is the *futurist*. This school of thought is often called *dispensationalist*, because of the underlying idea that Christian history can be divided into several dispensations, or periods of God's dealings with mankind.

Futurists believe that the major part of Revelation will be fulfilled at the end of the age. Unlike the historicists, they take the various time measurements literally. So they believe that just prior to the Lord's return there will be a seven-year tribulation period, probably divided into two periods of three and a half years each (1260 days).

As with the historicist view, the seven churches of chapters two and three are seen as representing seven periods of history leading up to the rapture of the Church. All the rest of the book, however, applies to the great tribulation, the triumph and return of Christ

FUTURIST SCHOOL OF INTERPRETATION

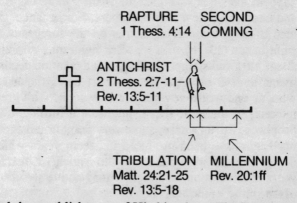

and the establishment of His kingdom. The Beast and the False prophet are literal, individual figures, who rise up at the end of the age in a final act of defiance against God.

There are minor differences of opinion within the futurist school - for instance, some see the rapture as taking place in the beginning and others at the middle of the tribulation.

Futurists generally tie the books of Daniel and

Revelation closely together. The idea of the huge time span between chapter three and the rest of the Apocalypse, for instance, is partly based on the seventieth week of the prophecy in Daniel chapter nine. Here, say the futurists, there is a gap of indeterminate length between weeks 69 and 70 (eg Pentecost, 1981, pp. 240ff). This week of years is clearly seen as a parallel to the seven years mentioned in Revelation.

The strength of this theory lies in the fact that the events so described could occur any time and, people are kept on their toes, as it were, in expectation. Also, because everything is future, there is great scope for the use of the imagination in trying to predict what will happen. This tends to make futurism a more exciting and interesting view than the others. For instance, the idea of people receiving marks on the foreheads or right hands (13:16), has spawned numerous rumours about infra-red stamping at banks and taxation departments and so on. Any news report of earthquakes, wars or one world government is watched with great interest, in the hope that it might be a fulfilment of prophecy. Furthermore, some very graphic and exciting films have been produced in recent years which depict horrific presentations of the Antichrist, fearful years of tribulation, and highly imaginative scenarios of the climax of the age.

The futurist view, on the other hand, like the praeterist, has the weakness that if it only applies to one generation of mankind; it is largely irrelevant to all the rest. It also makes some huge assumptions - for instance, that of the Church being raptured before the tribulation, which is not mentioned at all in the book of Revelation. Further, it tends to be selective in its methods of interpretation. The reference to marking the hand or the forehead in chapter 13 is usually taken literally, but the description of the Beast, earlier in the chapter, as having seven heads and ten horns, is taken symbolically. There do not seem to be any consistent guidelines for deciding which approach to adopt - a rather arbitrary choice seems the norm.

At least one historicist writer claims that futurism as a school of thought, was developed by a Spanish Jesuit, who wanted to come up with an alternative to the prevailing post-Reformation view that the pope was the antichrist. His name was Francisco Ribera, who wrote a commentary on the Apocalypse in 1585. This was reportedly published in 1838 by one Samuel Roffey Maitland in England (Foster, p.48f). So far, I have been unable to confirm this claim. One comment can be made, however, and that is that the basic ideas of futurism were clearly outlined by several of the Fathers hundreds of years before Ribera. The best example is probably to be found in the writings of Irenaeus, who was a second century bishop (*Against Heresies,* chapters 24-30). So whatever developments Ribera may have made in futurist thought, he can hardly be credited with having initiated it! He was well over a thousand years too late for that.

The futurist view is widespread among evangelical and pentecostal believers. Few scholarly Bible commentators seem comfortable with it, however, and by and large its advocacy is limited to the more 'popular' writers.

Fourthly, there is the *idealist* school. This view is that the Revelation does not refer to specific events, so much as to principles of God's dealing in the life of His people, and the continued conflict with the forces of evil. One great message comes through - the ultimate victory is the Lord's! So it does not matter whether the Antichrist is a Roman emperor, the papacy, a communist dictator, or a Muslim ayatollah,

- in whatever form he comes, and with however many 'heads' or 'crowns', he will never succeed. In the end, God will have the last word.

The strength of the idealist view lies in the fact that it is always relevant to every generation and is always applicable to any group of people who need encouragement. There is no need for historical knowledge or scholarship to find blessing in the book. So

IDEALIST SCHOOL OF INTERPRETATION

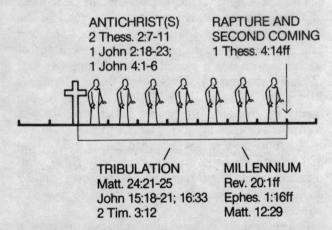

ANTICHRIST(S)
2 Thess. 2:7-11
1 John 2:18-23;
1 John 4:1-6

RAPTURE AND
SECOND COMING
1 Thess. 4:14ff

TRIBULATION
Matt. 24:21-25
John 15:18-21; 16:33
2 Tim. 3:12

MILLENNIUM
Rev. 20:1ff
Ephes. 1:16ff
Matt. 12:29

the letters to the seven churches, for example, can be uplifting to people of any church, at any time or place, even if they know nothing whatever about Ephesus or Smyrna or Philadelphia.

If the idealist view is taken too far, however, it avoids any literal application at all, and this would seem to be inconsistent with the nature of the Apocalypse. Real people, places and events are mentioned, and need to be recognised and understood wherever possible.

The idealist view may be found represented among Christians of all persuasions, and is increasingly popular in scholarly evangelical circles.

So far, I have only talked about the Book of Revelation. However, obviously, each school of thought has differing views of other areas of eschtology, too. For comparison, here are examples of the four views as applied to the tribulation and the Antichrist -

The Tribulation

Praeterist - the tribulation was centred at the fall of Jerusalem in AD 70 (Luke 21:20-24).
Historicist - the tribulation represents the whole gospel age (John 16:33; 2 Timothy 3:12).
Futurist - the tribulation will be a short time of intensive trouble at the end of the age (Revelation 7:14; 13:5).
Idealist - there will always be tribulation and trouble for the people of God, although it will vary in intensity from time to time and from place to place (John 16:33; 2 Timothy 3:12; Revelation 1:9).

The Antichrist

Praeterist - the Antichrist is a first century figure, possibly Nero. There was a myth of Nero Redivivus - that Nero would come back from the dead (Revelation 13:12).
Historicist - the papacy is the Antichrist as it takes the place of Christ in the thinking of many people (2

,1essalonians 2:4b).

Futurist - the Antichrist will be a powerful leader at the end of the age who will have a short-lived but terrifying rule (Revelation 13:5-17).

Idealist - there have always been Antichrists in the world and there always will be (1 John 2:18-23). No one particular Antichrist should be expected.

We will look at both the tribulation and the Antichrist in more detail later, but the above brief notes will serve to show how the different schools of thought see these subjects.

To conclude, it is obvious that there are good and godly people in all four schools of thought. They all have insights and understandings that are valid and valuable. No doubt, it is possible to hold to a combination of elements from each of them.

The most important thing is to be careful not to be too dogmatic or to suggest that one view is the only view. Tolerance and mutual respect are important.

(Note: Further details of each school of thought are given in the section on the Millennium.)

2. How can I understand the Book of Revelation?

The book of Revelation has always been a difficult one to understand. In fact, one cynic has suggested that it is the most ill-named book in the Bible! The renowned fourth century Church historian, Eusebius, pointed out that even in his day, there was some question about whether the book was canonical or not (*History,* 3, 25). Such notable persons as Luther and Zwingli queried whether it should even be in the New Testament at all (Bainton, 1984, p.332; Lenski, 1961, p.14).

The book is written in a literary style known as 'apocalyptic'. This word is based on the Greek verb *apokalupto* which means 'I reveal.' Apocalyptic books are usually full of visions and symbols which attempt to reveal divine mysteries. Parts of Daniel are presented in the same fashion. So, too, are sections of the book of Zechariah.

But these were just three of many such volumes in existence in the first century. For example, here is a list of some of the others -

Jewish Apocalyptic Books

- The Book of Enoch
- The Book of the Secrets of Enoch
- The Apocalypse of Baruch
- The Fourth Book of Esdras
- The Book of Jubilees
- The Assumption of Moses
- The Martyrdom of Isaiah
- The Psalms of Solomon
- The Apocalypse of Adam
- The Apocalypse of Elijah
- The Apocalypse of Zephaniah
- The Testament of the Twelve Patriarchs

Christian Apocalyptic Books

- The Apocalypse of Peter
- The Apocalypse of Paul
- The Apocalypse of John
- The Apocalypse of Thomas
- The Apocalypse of the Virgin
- The Apocalypse of Stephen
- The Apocalypse of James

There were several commonly accepted features of apocalyptic writing. Always, there was an acute expectation of the last days and the consummation of the age. Often, the writers used pseudonyms - especially of some well-known saint or prophetic figure. This was done in an endeavour to add credibility and authority to what they said. It was not dishonest, from their point of view, as they usually believed that what they wrote was consistent with the beliefs or convictions of the person whose name they adopted.

Apocalyptic writers always used symbolic language and normally presented their message in the form of visions. There was usually a messianic aspect to what they wrote, and the present evil age was commonly contrasted with the evil age to come. Final judgement was a continuing theme. A period of trouble was usually described as occurring just prior to the end of time and the ushering in of a golden age.

Obviously, the book of Revelation follows in this tradition. Many of the elements mentioned above may be found in it. However, there are some very distinct differences as well.

First of all, the author uses his own name, not that of another. (Since Eusebius' day, scholars have argued whether the writer was the apostle John or another John - it seems to me that there is adequate evidence that it was the apostle.)

Further, John openly gives the origin and destination of the book, and its emphasis is more on the kingdom of God than the kingdoms of this world.

Furthermore, there is no suggestion that the seer is using visions as a literary device. The visions are genuine revelations from God.

Swete puts it like this -

> The NT apocalypse alone stands in real relation to the life of the age in which it was written, or

attempts to reveal the meaning and issues of the events which the writer had witnessed or was able to foresee. The NT Apocalypse alone deserves the name or is in any true sense, a prophecy'. (1907, p.xxii)

In other words, Revelation does fall within the apocalyptic tradition, but it stands apart from it in several unique and important ways.

So why bother to talk about the apocalyptic tradition at all? Only to make the point that, just as the teachings of Paul are in letter form, and that knowing this helps us to understand them better, so some insight into the apoclyptic form helps us to understand the book of Revelation better.

We could describe the Apocalypse as being written in code language. In order to benefit from its message, we need to be able to crack the code. This is hinted at in the opening sentence of the book, which states that God 'made known' the revelation of Jesus Christ to John. This verb 'made known' is related to the word for 'sign'. It is used in the gospel of John to describe how Jesus tried to indicate to His disciples that He was going to be crucified (eg John 12:33; 18:32). In these cases, however, Jesus sometimes used symbolic, rather than direct language. In the same way, He spoke of Peter's death (John 21:19). Similarly, the verb is used of Agabus' prophecy about impending famine (Act 11:28).

Such symbolic language is quite typical of prophecy. In the Old Testament, in fact, it is clearly stated that prophets speak in visions, dreams and riddles (Numbers 12:6) A 'riddle' was usually a saying that had some hidden or subtle meaning that was not obvious at first. In fact, sometimes its meaning would not be known at all until the matter was fulfilled.

Hosea uses the word 'parable' (12:10). In other words, a presentation of God's word in a way that would require some kind of interpretation. Hosea's own prophecy is an example - his profligate wife is a symbol of unfaithful Israel (see chapters 1-3). Probably the best Old Testament example is that of Nathan, who used a parable to confront King David with his sin (2 Samuel 12:1ff).

The use of this verb right at the beginning of the Apocalypse makes it clear that here we have a volume that is presented in prophetic style in symbolic form.

Furthermore, the noun 'sign' is used elsewhere in the book to describe visions that John saw. For example, there is 'a woman clothed with the sun, with the moon under her feet and a crown of twelve stars' (Revelation 12:1). Obviously, there is no way that this vision can be taken literally! But to ensure that we understand this, John calls it a 'sign'.

Similarly, the dragon of verse three of the same chapter is a sign - in this case, one that is explained further in the passage (v.9).

In chapter 15, John tells us of a 'great and marvellous signs' (v.1). This involves seven angels and seven plagues and all the events that happen in the next three chapters.

If these are all signs, then they must depict something different from the actual things and happenings that they describe. A sign cannot be the same as the thing it signifies. We shall consider this later in regard to Armageddon, for instance, which is mentioned in chapter 16. Is this a literal battle or is it, in fact, a symbolic description of a spiritual conflict? Remember that it is a sign, not an actual event.

Another way of looking at this is to consider prophetic language as code language.

Usually, in a code, one symbol represents another.

For example, a series of dots and dashes may signify letters as in Morse code. Or, certain words may be used to give different designations to letters of the alphabet - unless you know what they are, the message is meaningless.

In Revelation, something similar applies. Take the first chapter, for instance. Here there is a dramatic picture of the risen, ascended Christ.

> I turned and saw seven golden lampstands, and among the lampstands was someone 'like a son of man,' dressed in a robe reaching down to his feet and with a golden sash around his chest. His head and his hair were white like wool, as white as snow, and his eyes were like blazing fire. His feet were like bronze glowing in a furnace, and his voice was like the sound of rushing waters. In his right hand he held seven stars, and out of his mouth came a sharp double- edged sword. His face was like the sun shining in all its brilliance.
>
> (Revelation 1:12-16)

Clearly, we are not expected to take all of this literally. The description is highly symbolical. An obvious example is the sword in the Lord's mouth. This clearly symbolises the word of God (Ephesians 6:17; Hebrews 4:12). Similarly, the next few verses tell us that the lampstands are churches and the stars are the 'angels' or messengers of the churches (Revelation 1:20).

Furthermore, the word 'mystery' is used to describe this symbolism (Revelation 1:20; 17:7). In Greek this word is very similar - it is *musterion* - but it really has a meaning closer to our word 'secret'. A *musterion* was a matter which was hidden but which could be made known to the initiated or informed. Many Greek religions were called 'mystery religions' because only when you were initiated and became one of the 'mustai' could you be admitted to the secret rites, which, were often quite immoral. In contrast to this, the apostle Paul describes the Christian faith as a - *musterion* which was hidden for ages, but which was made known through the coming of Christ and the teaching of the apostles and prophets (Ephesians 3:1-

THE BOOK OF REVELATION

A 'MYSTERY' — WRITTEN IN CODE
(Rev. 1:20; 17:7)

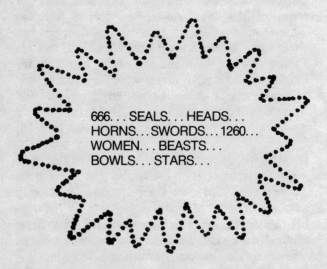

666. . . SEALS. . . HEADS. . .
HORNS. . . SWORDS. . . 1260. . .
WOMEN. . . BEASTS. . .
BOWLS. . . STARS. . .

'This calls for wisdom' (Rev. 13:18)

11; Colossians 1:25-27). By faith, anyone can be let into the secret!

In the Apocalypse, things are also presented in a *musterion*. But the secrets can be made known to those who understand the code.

There were practical reasons for this, too. Imagine

you were a Roman soldier, for instance. You are in-
structed to destroy all Christian scrolls and writings
that you find when you search a suspected Christian
home. If you find a book that says that the Roman
Empire will be destroyed, that the Emperor will be
brought low and that Christ will be King, you will naturally see it as seditious and deal with it - and its
owners - with great severity. On the other hand, if this
book is simply a strange collection of tales about
people with swords in their mouths, beasts with numerous heads and horns, great red dragons, complicated
sets of numbers and so on, you will probably dismiss it
as incomprehensible nonsense.

Of course, Romans soldiers were not on their own!
It is seemingly incomprehensible to many people
today as well! (Which is one reason why Luther had
questions about its place in the canon.) The greatest
problem that we face now is to identify the key to the
code. However, the most helpful thing is to realise that
there is a code - or in other words, to realise that the
book is presented in figurative form. Too often, we try
to interpret literally what should be taken symbolically. Examples of this will crop up as we go along, but
for now let's consider a couple of simple ones.

In chapter 13, there is a reference to the Beast
forcing people to receive a mark on the right hand or
on the forehead. There is a widespread belief that this
is to be taken literally. Some suggest that it will be
necessary before much longer to have such a mark,
before you can withdraw money from the bank or start
a new job and so on. Yet everything else in this
chapter is obviously symbolical. The Beast itself, for
instance, has seven heads and ten horns. These cannot
be taken literally. There is a dragon - obviously
representing the devil. There is a second beast - else-

where called the False Prophet - who has horns like a lamb. And so on.

Clearly, all of this must be reinterpreted into a feasible and realistic form. So if these aspects are to be taken as figurative, it is only consistent to take the description of bodily marking in the same way. It seems to me that what the passage means is that the Antichrist will make every effort to control human livelihood (the right hand) and human freedom of thought (the forehead). And there have been plenty of examples of this, of course, ever since the days of Rome.

I am not suggesting that seeing the book as essentially metaphorical, rather than literal, will make it possible to understand everything in it. In fact, I have many questions myself about some of the symbolism used. But it will help us to avoid some of the more bizarre and fanciful interpretations, that in the long run turn people away from a serious consideration of this dramatic part of the Bible.

Further, there are many similarities between the Old Testament and Revelation. A study of Ezekiel or Daniel is often helpful in understanding the Apocalypse. For instance, the background to chapter 13 of Revelation seems to lie partly in Daniel chapter seven. The beast which John describes there combines features of all of the beasts of which Daniel writes.

Finally, I believe there is a reason for the symbolic language in Revelation. If the book was presented in such a way that every detail was literally fulfilled, there could only be one possible application to one series of historical events. Once this had occurred, the book would have little relevance for anyone else. As it is, it can, in fact, be applied over and over again to troublesome situations. Whether it be a persecuted Christian in the second century in North Africa, a

Chinese believer suffering under communist oppression in the 1950's, or an Iranian saint being imprisoned for his faith in the 1980's, the message of the Apocalypse is relevant. The 'Beast' might be enjoying a short time of power. But this will be only like the three and a half years of Ahab's tyranny in the days of Elijah, or of the reign of Antiochus Epiphanes in the times of the Maccabees. He might be controlling people's work life and thought life. He may be acting like God! But his days are numbered and the Lord will bring him down. The ultimate triumph is the Lord's, who will come like a rider on a white horse, conquering his foes and establishing His kingdom in victory!

This is the message of the Apocalypse. It is a timeless theme, always meaningful and always encouraging.

> Now have come the salvation and the power and the kingdom of our God, and the authority of His Christ.
> For the accuser of our brothers ... has been hurled down.
> They overcame him by the blood of the Lamb and by the word of their testimony;
> they did not love their lives so much as to shrink from death.
> Therefore rejoice, you heavens and you who dwell in them!
>
> (Revelation 12:10-12)

3. What is the Great Tribulation?

The view you hold of the tribulation largely depends on whether you are a praeterist, a historicist, a futurist or an idealist! Perhaps the reverse is also true - your understanding of the tribulation decides what school of thought you belong to.

Praeterists basically believe the tribulation was the time of Roman persecution of believers. Historicists see it as covering the whole gospel age. Futurists believe it is still to come. Idealists see it as covering the whole gospel age, but with special reference to particular periods or locations where persecution has been intense.

The most popular view among charismatic and evangelical believers is the futurist. In simple terms, this is the belief that there will be an intense period of seven years of tribulation immediately prior to the end of the age. This concept is based initially on the words of Jesus in Matthew 24, where, in the language of the Authorised Version of the Bible, He said, 'For then shall be great tribulation, such as was not since the beginning of the world to this time, no, nor ever shall be' (verse 21).

Jesus also referred to the 'abomination of desolation' being erected in the holy place (verse 15) and went on to say that 'immediately after the tribulation of those days' signs would appear in the heavens indicating His return (verse 29).

Similarly, the prophet Daniel also spoke of 'desolations' prior to the end and of an 'abomination that causes desolation' (Daniel 9:26,27).

Furthermore, if the letters to the seven churches of Revelation are taken as depicting seven eras of history, the church of Philadelphia represents the second to last period. To that church, the Lord says that He will keep them from the 'hour of trial that is going to come upon the whole world' (Revelation 3:10).

Then, in the 13th chapter of Revelation, there is a graphic description of the tyranny of the Beast who reigns for 42 months (that is, three and a half years). This is seen by some as an intensifying of the seven-year tribulation period - and hence called the 'great' tribulation.

When we look closely at the teachings of Jesus, however, we see that the context of His statements about tribulation is actually the fall of Jerusalem in AD 70 when, according to Josephus, 'every sort of death was thought more tolerable than the famine' (*Wars,* 6,7,2) and tens of thousands of Jewish people perished.

This is indicated more clearly in Luke who quotes Jesus as saying that there would be great distress 'in the land', that is, in Palestine (21:23), after which Jerusalem would be taken captive and trampled on by the Gentiles.

Furthermore, the rest of the New Testament indicates that tribulation and distress would be the ongoing, continuous lot of the people of God (John 15:18f; 2 Timothy 3:12). It is interesting that in his introduction to the Apocalypse, John describes himself as 'your brother and companion in suffering' (1:9). Literally, the last two words could be rendered as 'in the tribulation', which suggests that John saw himself as in it then.

In chapter seven of Revelation, we see the tribulation spoken of as an age-long affair. John sees a vision of a crowd of people so great that it cannot be counted. They come from every nation, tribe, people and language. When John asks who they are, he is given this answer -

> These are they who have come out of the great tribulation; they have washed their robes and made them white in the blood of the Lamb. Therefore,
> 'they are before the throne of God
> and serve Him day and night in his temple;

and he who sits on the throne will spread his tent
over them.
Never again will they hunger;
never again will they thirst.
The sun will not beat upon them,
nor any scorching heat.
For the Lamb at the centre of the throne will
be their shepherd;
he will lead them to springs of living water.
And God will wipe away every tear from their
eyes.'

(Revelation 7:14ff)

There seems little doubt that this is a description of
all the people of God from all generations and nations.
Yet all of them are described as having come out of the
great tribulation. This seems to suggest that while
there was a specific time of distress prophesied by
Jesus which took place at the Roman conquest of
Jerusalem, there was also a larger sense in which there
would always be tribulation of one kind or another for
the people of God. Similarly, Revelation 13:10 calls
for patience and endurance on the part of the saints in
the face of tribulation.

What about the time periods of seven years and
three and a half years? Hendriksen makes the useful
suggestion that we should draw a comparison between
the days of Elijah and Ahab and the events spoken of
in the Apocalypse (1986, p. 143). In Elijah's day there
was a drought for three and half years. It was a time
when the people of God were persecuted and yet the
word of the Lord was proclaimed (see 1 Kings 17 and
18). Through it all, true believers were protected and
nourished.

A comparison of Revelation 11:6 and James 5:17
indicates the validity of this view.

This is not to say that we should expect a literal period of three and a half years of distress at the end of the age. Remember that Revelation is a book of symbols - almost everything has a hidden meaning. It is to say, however, that just as there was a time of oppression, persecution and distress in Elijah's day, so throughout the gospel age, there will be trouble and distress for God's people.

During Ahab's reign, however, a faithful remnant survived - seven thousand, in fact, had refused to bow the knee to Baal (1 Kings 19:18). Moreover, at the end of that cruel time, there was a great victory for the people of God and the Lord's triumph was displayed. First of all, there was Elijah's encounter with the prophets of Baal on Mount Carmel (1 Kings 18:20ff), and then the decimation of the house of Ahab (1 Kings 22:1ff; 2 Kings 9:1ff). Similarly, there will be a final triumph for the Lord's new covenant people at the end of the age, and the establishing of the eternal kingdom of God.

Finally, we must be very careful not to interpret Scripture only in the context of our own time and culture. It is very easy for us, in our cosy Western middle-class society, to talk of some future time of tribulation as if it had not yet occurred.

What of the tens of thousands of believers who have experienced distress over the centuries - deprivation, imprisonment, starvation, hard labour, torture and death? In early 1987, Dr David Barrett, whose *World Christian Encyclopaedia* is the definitive textbook on the extent of Christianity around the world, claimed that on average, 330,000 believers are martyred every year! He estimated that one in every 200 evangelists, pastors and missionaries were currently being martyred for the faith. An estimated 500,000 lost their lives in Uganda alone in recent years.

For those people, great tribulation is a very present reality. How could it get any worse? What more could be done to them?

A balanced view of Scripture and history seems to lead us to the conclusion that while the Lord did talk of intense suffering within a generation of His own day, He also warned us that there would always be such times and He encouraged us to believe that one way or the other, whether through life or through death, God would deliver us.

4. What is the Rapture?

The word 'rapture' comes from the past participle of the Latin verb *rapere* which means 'to snatch' or 'to sieze'. The word does not occur in the Bible, but the event which it describes does.

The rapture is the taking away of believers from the earth at the return of the Lord. The Lord Jesus foretold that at His coming He would send out His angels who would gather His people from the four corners of the earth (Matthew 24:31). Paul also described how we would be caught up to meet the Lord in the air at His return (1 Thessalonians 4:17). The verb which Paul uses here *(harpadzo)* is a strong one. It means to seize hastily or to snatch by sudden, violent movement.

Luke uses it, for instance, to describe how Paul was rescued from a mob by a band of Roman soldiers (Acts 23:10). Similarly, when Jesus said that God's kingdom was coming forcefully, and that forceful people would grasp hold of it (Matthew 11:12), He used the same verb. Again, in the parable of the sower, the devil 'snatches away' what is sown in the heart - the verb is *harpadzo* (Matthew 13:19). And Jude encourages us to 'snatch' people from the fire in order to save them (verse 23).

Most interesting of all is the use of the verb to describe how the Spirit of the Lord 'suddenly took Philip away' from the road to Gaza and left him many miles north-west at Azotus (Acts 8:39). This is probably the nearest to the concept of the rapture of the Church at the end of the age. Just as the Spirit took hold of Philip and simply transported him to another place, so will the Lord, at His parousia, take His people from this weary earth to meet Him in the air.

Most Christian believers agree about the fact of the rapture. There are several differing opinions about the time and manner of it.

Some are of the opinion that the rapture will occur seven years and others three and a half years before the Lord actually appears. This is often referred to as a 'secret' rapture because people will just disappear without warning. There will be immediate world-wide chaos as air traffic controllers vanish, train drivers and pilots disappear, and workers in industry and commerce are suddenly nowhere to be seen and so on. Those who remain will be bewildered, confused, panic-stricken. Naturally, there will be carnage and death as planes and trains crash, essential utilities cease to function properly, and children and spouses are left inexplicably alone.

Then will follow the time of tribulation and the reign of the Antichrist.

This is a very dramatic scenario and it has promoted some very exciting books and gospel films - and indeed has led many people to Christ.

The Scriptural basis for it is seen initially in the teaching of Jesus, where He spoke of two people being in the same room or at the same work bench, and one being taken while the other is left (Matthew 24:36-41).

According to some, the marriage supper of the

Lamb will take place over the intervening period until the Lord comes (Revelation 19:9).

Then, when the Lord returns, He will come 'with all His holy ones' (1 Thessalonians 3:13) - in other words, the raptured saints. He will 'bring with Him' those believers who have died previously (1 Thessalonians 4:14).

Furthermore, there are many promises in Scripture that believers will be saved from the wrath to come (Romans 5:9; Ephesians 2:1ff).

When we look at the context of Jesus' teaching, however, we find that what He said about one person being taken and one being left is actually a reference to people being taken in judgement.

Just as the flood came and took people away in Noah's day, so at the parousia, some (the ungodly) will be taken and others (believers) will be left. This passage indicates that God's wrath will be displayed against sinners before, or at least at the same time as, the Lord comes for His saints.

In the parable of the wheat and the weeds, we see something similar.

> As the weeds are pulled up and burned in the fire, so it will be at the end of the age. The Son of Man will send out his angels, and they will weed out of his kingdom everything that causes sin and all who do evil. They will throw them into a fiery furnace, where there will be weeping and gnashing of teeth. Then the righteous will shine like the sun in the kingdom of their Father.
>
> (Matthew 13:40ff)

The order of events is very clear here. First the wicked are dealt with and then the righteous remain. Meanwhile, 'both grow together until the harvest' (Matthew 13:30). This does not seem to allow for a

144

catching away of believers before the Lord comes in judgement on sinners - indeed, the very opposite is clearly indicated.

When we look at Paul's teaching in his two letters to the Thessalonians, we find a similar pattern. Indeed, we look in vain for even the slightest hint of the Church being raptured before the coming of the Lord in judgement on the ungodly.

In the first letter, the gathering of the saints occurs when the Lord descends 'with a loud command, with the voice of the archangel and with the trumpet call of God' (4:16). This same trumpet call is referred to in 1 Corinthians as the 'last' trumpet (15:52). If it is the last one, then there can be no other to follow. The gathering of the people of God is obviously the final aspect of the Lord's return.

Also, the reference to Christ bringing those who have fallen asleep with Him is not a reference to the parousia at all. Here Paul is talking about the resurrection. Just as God brought Jesus back from the dead, so He will bring believers back from the dead with Him (4:14). In fact, this is really Paul's subject here - what happens to Christians after death. The first point that he makes is that they do not stay dead! Like Jesus, they will rise again! It is only in the next verse that Paul begins to talk about the return of Christ.

Finally, he says that all believers, both living and dead, will go 'to meet the Lord in the air' (4:17). The word here translated as 'meet' could possibly be rendered as 'greet'. It was a technical term used in antiquity to describe a public welcome that might be given to an important visitor by the civic leaders of a city. Usually, just as they would do today, such leaders would meet the dignitary concerned and then escort him back into the city for a banquet or civic reception of some kind. So they would both 'meet' him and 'greet' him. The same expression is used of the brides-maids in the parable Jesus told of the wedding reception. The young ladies were waiting to 'meet' the bridegroom when he came to the wedding reception (Matthew 25:1). They would greet him and then escort him immediately into the banquet hall. Similarly, Luke tells how when he and Paul arrived in Rome, some of the brothers travelled some 70 kilometres out of the city to meet them and then to return with them (Acts 28:15).

In the same way, we shall both meet and greet the Lord in the air, and then come back to the earth with Him as He establishes His kingdom here! There is no suggestion of going away with Him for a few years and then returning with Him! It all happens as one event.

Similarly, in Paul's second letter to the Thessalonians, he describes in vivid terms Christ's coming 'in blazing fire' to judge the ungodly, 'on the day when he comes to be glorified in his holy people' (1:7-9). Both the outpouring of God's wrath on sinners and the final redemption of believers are described as contemporaneous. There is no suggestion of believers having been removed a few years earlier.

And as for the book of Revelation, Dr. W.G. Scroggie, himself a believer in the 'secret rapture', declared that the rapture was an event 'of which the seer of Patmos says nothing' (1981, p.381ff).

Furthermore, with some writers, there is an unfortunate confusion between tribulation and suffering for believers, and the judgement and wrath of God on unbelievers (eg Petree, Stanton). Naturally, if you can argue that the 'tribulation' is a time of punishment for the ungodly, it is logical that God's people can have no part of it. This is an assumption, however, that has little biblical basis. Clearly, in any time of tribulation, it may well be that saint and sinner alike suffer (as in the imprisonment of dissidents in the Soviet Union, where all who refuse to embrace communism, whether Christian or non-Christian, may find themselves in trouble). However, the emphasis in the Bible seems, if anything, to lean in the other direction - namely, that the believers are the ones who are likely to experience hardship and pain.

This is why Jesus clearly promised that the days of distress would be cut short for the sake of the elect (Matthew 24:22). And Paul, having talked about the rise of the 'man of sin' encourages his readers to 'stand firm' (2 Thessalonians 2:15).

One's view of this is largely determined by one's view of Israel. If we see end-time events being centred around the nation of Israel, then our view of the Antichrist, the tribulation and the rapture is necessarily different. If, however, we see the Church as the centre of God's ultimate plan for the world, then the view that I am presenting here is the obvious one. We will look at this issue in more detail elsewhere.

Finally, let's consider the practical implications of the idea of Christians being raptured before the Tribulation. It sounds fine in a prosperous, Western church, to claim that before things get too tough, the Lord is going to take us all away. But how do you get on talking to prisoners in a Siberian labour camp, or to believers in a fire-gutted Ugandan village, or to sufferers in an Iranian jail?

Can you imagine the reaction if we were to stand before them and say, 'Cheer up! There is no need to worry. Before the tribulation comes, the Lord will rescue you so that you won't have to suffer.' Surely, they will respond with something like, 'What do you mean, 'before tribulation comes'? Surely we're in trouble now! Don't tell us it's going to become even worse!' One preacher used to say that if the Lord delivers twentieth century Western believers from tribulation, He will have a lot of apologising to do to the millions who have suffered torture and death for Christ in other places and in previous generations. Why should He deliver a select few, when so many others have been left to endure the worst that Satan can conceive?

As I mentioned above, many people have been converted through sincere and forthright preaching of the imminent rapture of the Church and the danger of being left behind. Praise the Lord for the way His Spirit generously uses the preaching of the gospel in spite of differing understandings of it.

But it seems to me that a consistent view of the Bible makes it clear that the whole of the gospel era is potentially a time of suffering for the people of God, and that the climax of the age on that great Day when He comes again is the hope to which we look.

5. Who is the Antichrist?

Who is the Antichrist? This is one of the most interesting and fascinating questions related to the return of the Lord Jesus Christ.

There are almost as many opinions about this as there are books and sermons on the subject! From the earliest times, there has been speculation and debate.

Some people seem to spend a great deal of time looking for a coming world ruler. A friend of mine once wrote an article about this. 'I'm looking for him, too,' he said. 'His name is Jesus.'

I wish I had written that!

Nevertheless, since the beginning of Christianity, there has always been someone trying to work out who the Antichrist is, when he will appear, what he will look like, where he will live and what his number means.

There was a popular myth in the late first century that the emperor Nero, who had died in AD 68 at the young age of 32, would reappear. Some thought that he was not really dead at all, but was in hiding somewhere. Others felt that he would actually rise from the dead. An early Christian martyr named Commodianus, who died around 240 AD, wrote, 'Nero shall be raised up from hell ... the whole earth on all sides, for seven years shall tremble' (*Instructions*, 41).

Irenaeus, who was bishop of Lyons in the second century, believed that the Antichrist would come from the tribe of Dan. He based this on a text in Jeremiah (8:16) and felt that the absence of the name of Dan from the list of tribes in Revelation chapter seven confirmed this (*Against Heresies*, 30,1).

Another early martyr, a vigorous and controversial theologian, and one-time leader of the church of Rome named Hippolytus (AD 170-235), followed the same line as Irenaeus (Treatise on Christ and Antichrist, 14).

During the Reformation, the Catholic Church was so corrupt many Reformers labelled the Pope as the Antichrist. Wyclif and Hus are obvious examples. In Hus' day, for example, there were at one time three popes, all claiming to be the true representative of Christ on earth! One of them, John XXIII, was described by Hus as 'a base murderer, a sodomite, a simoniac, and a heretic' (quoted in Budgen, 1983, p.241). The Church itself later renounced this man. But meanwhile Hus and his companions had no hesitation in talking of the papacy as the Antichrist (Budgen, 1983, p.112).

Similarly, Luther came reluctantly to the same view

(Bainton, 1978, 1984, p.109ff). Even in the Preface to the Authorised Version of the Bible, 'the most high and mighty prince James' is given credit for having 'dealt such a blow to that Man of Sin (ie the pope) as will not be healed.'

The Presbyterian Westminster Confession of 1648 declared -

> There is no other head of the church but the Lord Jesus Christ. Nor can the pope of Rome, in any sense, be head thereof; but is that Antichrist, that man of sin and son of perdition, that exalteth himself in the church against Christ, and all that is called God.
>
> (XXV, vi)

More recent editions of this Confession stop at the word 'thereof'! Times have clearly changed. But the belief of the seventeenth century puritans was very clear.

100 years later, Wesley was of a similar persuasion. In his *Notes on the New Testament,* Wesley plainly wrote, 'The Beast (ie the Antichrist) is the Romish Papacy' (on Revelation 13:1).

Others believe that the Antichrist only emerges at the end of the age. Again, this is no new idea. It occurs in the Fathers. One of the earliest Christian writings is a document called *The Didache* (pronounced did-ar-kay). The title means 'The Teaching' and it purports to summarise the teaching of the Apostles. Written in the mid second century, it deals with matters of Christian living and church practice. In its concluding passage, it says -

> Then the Deceiver of the World will show himself, pretending to be a Son of God and doing signs and wonders, and the earth will be delivered into his hands, and he will work such wickedness

150

as there has never been since the beginning. After that, all humankind will come up for fiery trial ... and then the whole world will see the Lord as He comes riding on the clouds of heaven.

Similarly, the great theologian Augustine wrote that there would be a 'last persecution' by the Antichrist and that the Lord Jesus Christ would 'kill Antichrist with the breath of His mouth' at His parousia (*City of God*, 20,12,13).

Over recent years, people like Stalin and Mussolini and Hitler and even Henry Kissinger (Smith, 1980) have all been suggested.

First of all, let's define our terms. The word 'Christ' comes from the Greek word *Christos* which means 'anointed one'. This, in turn, is a translation of the Hebrew word for 'messiah'. In its original usage, this word usually applied to a king who was 'anointed' to rule. David is the best example of this. He was anointed initially by Samuel the prophet (1 Samuel 16:1ff), and then again both by the people of Judah (2 Samuel 2:4) and Israel (2 Samuel 5:3). From that time on, kings were commonly referred to as 'anointed ones'. This is particularly evident in the Psalms (eg 2:2; 18:50; 89:38; 105:15; 132:10).

But there was more than this. There would be one divinely elected ruler in the lineage of David who would be anointed to reign forever over the house of Israel. His kingdom would never end (Isaiah 9:6,7). Indeed, the line of David would continue like the sun and the moon (Psalm 89:36f).

So before Jesus was born, it was promised that He would be such a sovereign. The Lord God would give to Him the throne of His father David and His kingdom would last forever (Luke 1:32f). In other words, He would be the Anointed One par excellence. He would be the Messiah, the Christ.

When the first of Jesus' disciples, Andrew, told his brother Simon about Him, he exclaimed, 'We have found the Messiah!' (John 1:41). And at the end of His ministry, mockingly, the inscription on the cross announced that Jesus was the 'King of the Jews' - or, in other words, the Messiah (John 19:19).

The 'anti' part of the word 'antichrist' is a Greek prefix which basically means, as it does in English, 'against' or 'opposed to'. However, it can also have connotations of 'instead of' or 'in place of'. In the word 'antichrist' it has both ideas. The Antichrist is someone who both stands opposed to and in the place of the Lord Jesus Christ.

The word is only used in the letters of John (1 John 2:18,22; 4:3; 2 John 7). However, it has universally been agreed since the writings of the Fathers that the 'man of sin' mentioned in Paul's second letter to the Thessalonians (2:3ff) and the Beast of Revelation (13:1ff) may also be identified as the personification of the Antichrist.

It is helpful to start with John. First of all, he points out clearly, that even in his own day, there was not just one antichrist, but many, and that they were already in the world!

> Dear children, this is the last hour; and as you have heard that the antichrist is coming, even now many antichrists have come.

(1 John 2:18)

Two things are clear in this passage. First of all, there was an expectation of one particular anti-Christian figure - 'the antichrist'. But there were also many lesser antichrists in existence.

John now goes on to describe the identifying characteristics of an antichrist figure -

1. He is pseudo-christian. The antichrists of John's

152

day had actually been in the church but 'they went out from us'. Ultimately, they could not stay because they really did not belong (1 John 2:19).

2. *He is a liar.* Those who know and obey the truth are followers of Christ. No antichrist can be part of the truth because, obviously, 'no lie comes from the truth' (1 John 2:21).

3. *He denies the Father and the Son.* John puts this *very plainly* -

> Who is a liar? It is the man who denies that Jesus is the Christ. Such a man is the antichrist - he denies the Father and the Son. No one who denies the Son has the Father; whoever acknowledges the Son has the Father also.
>
> (1 John 2:22f)

Clearly, no antichrist can recognise or admit that Jesus is Christ because this would be a self-defeating contradiction in terms. The whole point of the name 'antichrist', as we have seen, is that it describes someone who is clearly and unequivocally opposed to the Lord Jesus Christ - and who tries to usurp His position.

4. *He denies that Jesus was Christ in the flesh.* Indeed, this is how one may test truth from error.

> Dear friends, do not believe every spirit, but test the spirits to see whether they are from God, because many false prophets have gone out into the world. This is how you can recognise the Spirit of God: Every spirit that acknowledges that Jesus Christ has come in the flesh is from God, but every spirit that does not acknowledge Jesus is not from God. This is the spirit of the antichrist, which you have heard is coming and even now is already in the world.
>
> (1 John 4:1ff)

It is clear from this passage that a fundamental test of the genuineness of a theology is its understanding of the incarnation of Christ. Was Jesus really the Messiah? Was He really human? Was He from heaven?

A similar point is made in John's second letter -

> Many deceivers, who do not acknowledge Jesus Christ as coming in the flesh, have gone out into the world. Any such person is the deceiver and the antichrist.

> (2 John 7)

Of course, John is careful to say that such 'spirits' must be tested. It may well be that publicly, they in fact purport to believe in the Lord Jesus Christ. Note that he uses both the words 'liar' and 'deceiver' to describe the Antichrist. It is what really lies in the heart that counts.

This is how the Reformers could feel that a medieval pope could be an embodiment of the Antichrist. Nominally, his confession every time he celebrated mass was that Jesus was Christ in the flesh. In practice, however, the lifestyle of men like Alexander VI, the now rejected John XXIII, and Leo X bore no resemblance to the truth to which they paid lip service on Sundays in the cathedral.

Paul's description of the 'man of sin' indicates a similar situation. Once again, we have a picture of a person who may outwardly seem to be a Christian but who is actually deeply and fervently opposed to Christ. Here is what Paul says -

> Concerning the coming of our Lord Jesus Christ and our being gathered to him, we ask you, brothers, not to become easily alarmed by some prophecy, report or letter supposed to have come from us saying that the day of the Lord has already

come. Don't let anyone deceive you in any way, for that day will not come until the rebellion occurs and the man of lawlessness is revealed, the man doomed to destruction,

He will oppose and will exalt himself over everything that is called God or is worshipped, so that he sets himself up in God's temple, proclaiming himself to be God.

(2 Thessalonians 2:1ff)

It is interesting that there seem to be two contradictory factors here. On the one hand, the 'man of lawlessness' sets himself up in God's temple - that is, the church - and yet on the other hand, he exalts himself above every other object of worship, including God.

There is a further fascinating aspect as well. Paul describes the Antichrist as 'the man doomed to destruction' - a phrase better known in its Authorised Version form 'the son of perdition'. This is identical to the phrase Jesus used to describe Judas Iscariot! (John 17:12). Judas, again, was one who appeared to be a disciple of Christ, yet who was in his heart antagonistic to the kingdom of God.

Paul goes on to make some further points about this personage -

And now you know what is holding him back, so that he may be revealed at the proper time. For the secret power of lawlessness is already at work; but the one who now holds it back will continue to do so till he is taken out of the way.

And then the lawless one will be revealed, whom the Lord Jesus will overthrow with the breath of his mouth and destroy by the splendour of his coming (parousia). The coming of the lawless one will be in accordance with the work of Satan displayed in all kinds of counterfeit miracles, signs and wonders, and in every sort of evil that deceives those who are perishing. They perish because they refused to love the truth and so be saved. For this reason God sends them a powerful delusion so that they will believe the lie and so that all will be condemned who have not believed the truth but have delighted in wickedness.

(2 Thessalonians 2:6ff)

Many interesting points emerge here once again. In summarising what Paul says, we can list the following characteristics of the man of lawlessness -

1. The man of lawlessness will be revealed prior to the return of the Lord (v.3). Indeed, Christ cannot return until this has happened.

2. His nature is lawless (v.3). The very essence of this man is that he will be antagonistic to all order, decency and moral stability.

3. He is doomed to destruction (v.3). No matter what he does, his fate is already sealed. There is no hope for him. Destruction is his 'father', as it were, and he cannot escape his destiny.

4. He will oppose all that is godly (v.4). He will not be able to abide anything that is above him - he alone desires to be worshipped. He will not even allow God to be exalted above him.

5. He will ultimately install himself in the very Church itself and then call himself God! (v.4) These claims seem extraordinary, and it is unclear how they can come to pass. But one way or another, they will identify the Antichrist.

6. He will perform counterfeit signs, wonders and miracles (v.9). This will be a particularly troublesome area, because many people will not be able to distinguish between true and false wonders. The horrific story of Jim Jones who led nearly one thousand people to suicide a few years ago, because they were deluded by the apparent miracles which he performed, is well known. Such things can happen.

7. *He will deceive those those who refuse to love the truth* (v.10f). Just as John described the Antichrist as a deceiver, so Paul also says that people will be led astray by him. It is noteworthy that only those who refuse the truth will be affected. If we are committed to integrity and choose what is right, regardless, we will not be deceived. It is also interesting that Paul draws a contrast, not only between truth and error, but also between truth and wickedness (v.12). In the Bible, truth is not only knowing the right things, it is also doing the right things. In other words, those who want to do what is right are unlikely to be led astray by error. Even if they don't know a lot, they usually know what is right!

There is one puzzling part of all that Paul says about this man of iniquity. This 'secret power of lawlessness' is already at work, he writes, but it is also being restrained until the one who holds it back is removed and then it will be revealed. To the Thessalonians he says, 'You know what is holding him back' (v.6). We are not so fortunate. No one today can be really sure whether he knows or not! Fifteen hundred years ago, the learned Augustine wrote, 'I frankly confess I do not know what he means' (*City of God*, 20,19). More recently, the renowned Australian scholar, Leon Morris, said exactly the same thing! (1959, p.227).

There are several possible options. Augustine quotes one suggestion that the Roman Empire was the restraining force. When the Empire's stable government was removed, then the Antichrist would appear. Other ideas that he mentions are that the man of sin was presumed dead in Paul's day, but that he would appear again, once the restraint of his seclusion was removed.

Another idea was that he was just waiting until there were enough wicked defectors from the church, which John describes as being antichrists, for him to mount a formidable challenge to God (*City of God*, 20, 19).

Hendriksen simply argues for natural law and order, which prevents a man of lawlessness from emerging (1955, 1974, p.182).

There have been other suggestions that the restraining power is the Holy Spirit, who will be withdrawn from the earth at the beginning of a great seven-year tribulation at the end of the age (eg White, 1970). Few scholarly commentators seem inclined to this view, however. Futurists usually opt for it, as it fits in well with their overall scenario. It is a little disappointing, nevertheless, to see perhaps the most lucid advocate of futurism choosing this view, partly because on a process of elimination, it is the only option left (Pentecost, 1981, p.262).

Most commentators wisely admit, like Augustine, that no one knows. Certainly, Paul describes the '*secret* power of lawlessness' and perhaps this phrase in itself is enough to warn us not to speculate too much!

A couple of other comments may still be made. It is interesting that in 2 Thessalonians 2:6 the Greek grammar makes the restraining power a neuter force whereas in verse 7 it is masculine. Does this imply both an individual and a system?

Also, the verb translated as 'hold back' could possibly mean to 'hold fast' or to 'hold sway'. In this case, there could be a suggestion of Satanic domination over the Antichrist figure until such time as he desired to allow him to come forward. Certainly, we know that the Antichrist derives his power from Satan (see Revelation 13:2). So perhaps this is what Paul means.

In the final analysis, however, we really can't be sure.

The other passage that deals with the Antichrist is Revelation chapter 13. Here, he is depicted as a 'Beast'. This is the subject of the next section.

6. Who is the Beast and what is his mark?

(Note: See the previous section on the Antichrist before reading this section.)

If the identity of the Antichrist has aroused widespread interest, the nature of the Beast has stirred equal speculation! The Beast is one of the most intriguing, awesome, horrific, creepy creatures mentioned in the Bible. Here is how the Book of Revelation describes him -

> And I saw a beast coming out of the sea. He had ten horns and seven heads, with ten crowns on his horns, and on each head a blasphemous name. The beast I saw resembled a leopard, but had feet like those of a bear and a mouth like that of a lion. The dragon gave the beast his power and his throne and great authority. One of the heads of the beast seemed to have a fatal wound, but the fatal wound had been healed. The whole world was astonished and followed the beast. Men worshipped the dragon because he had given authority to the beast and asked, 'Who is like the beast? Who can make war against him?'
>
> The beast was given a mouth to utter proud words and blasphemies and to exercise his authority for forty-two months. He opened his mouth to blaspheme God, and to slander his name and his dwelling place and those who live in heaven. He

was given power to make war against the saints and to conquer them. And he was given authority over every tribe, people, language and nation. All inhabitants of the earth will worship the beast - all whose names have not been written in the book of life belonging to the Lamb that was slain from the creation of the world ...

This calls for patient endurance and faithfulness on the part of the saints.

(Revelation 13:1-10)

Clearly, this passage is highly symbolic. Almost everything in it is figurative. Symbols always represent something different from the symbol. So the fact that the Antichrist is called a Beast means in fact that this is the one thing he cannot be - a literal beast. What it means is that he is in some ways *like* the Beast described. So without going into detail we can note a couple of obvious meanings. First of all, he comes out of the sea. Probably, he comes gradually, and John may well have been appalled as he saw first the shining crowns, then the horrible heads, followed by the leopard's body and then the awesome bear's feet. Perhaps, it was only at this point that the creature roared, for John mentions his mouth 'like that of a lion' last of all.

Leon Morris suggests that the sea represents a pool of evil from which the Beast rises (1983, p.165). Others suggest that it is a reference in fact to the peoples of the world - and that it is from the nations themselves that this new and tyrannical leader emerges (cf Revelation 17:15). He rises from among them in order to rule over them.

In Daniel's prophecy, there are four beasts. Here, they are all rolled into one. Daniel's lion represents the empire of Babylon (Daniel 7:17ff). The bear is Medo-Persia, which overcame Babylon. Then the eagle is Greece, whose lightning conquest under Alexander the Great swept across the world like the flight of an eagle. Finally, there is the Beast itself which reflects the terrible, unnamed creature of Daniel 7 (vv 19ff).

What we see here, then, is not just one empire, but many; not just one ruler, but an amalgamation of several; not one particular kingdom, but the epitome and embodiment of all tyranny and corruption.

The seven heads and ten crowned horns indicate wide ranging authority - indeed, there are more crowns than heads, suggesting that this beast has usurped powers that are not rightfully his. The numbers seven and ten line up clearly with Paul's assertion that the Antichrist calls himself God - both are numbers that elsewhere in Scripture are clearly divine (eg the seven days of creation; the 'seven spirits of God'; the ten commandments).

The Beast's power is of Satanic origin (13:2). More than that, he has an apparently fatal wound from which he recovers. This pseudo-miracle is obviously an imitation of the genuine death that the Lord Jesus Christ suffered on the cross, and of the genuine resurrection to new life which He demonstrated.

Nevertheless, whatever this apparent come-back is, it causes 'the whole world' to be astonished and to worship the Beast (13:3,4). Again, this simply echoes what Paul says.

Furthermore, the fatal wound suggestfs a *perpetual rejuvenative power* possessed by the Beast. Take the Roman Empire, for instance, which was clearly uppermost in the minds of John and his readers. The day would come when it would suffer fatal harm. But this would not mark the end of the Beast. He would simply rise again in another form.

And this is what history has shown. Satanic power declines in one area only to rise again in another. In our own time, for example, we have seen the rise and fall of Nazism followed immediately by the upsurge of communism around the world.

At different times, many Christians have felt that either of these tyrannies could be embodiments of the power of the Beast. However, now we seen an even more frightening force emerging - the petro-dollar backed spread of Islam.

No sooner is an evil power defeated in one area than it arises in a different form in another. The deadly wound is healed not just once, but over and over again. So the Beast always seems to have a fatal wound which has been healed (13:3). No wonder people ask, 'Who is like the Beast? Who can make war against him?' (verse 4).

The Beast is given authority for 42 months. Many people take this literally and see a three and a half year reign for the Antichrist at the end of the age. Indeed, this idea is a very ancient one and can be found in the writings of the Fathers. Towards the end of the second century, Irenaeus, for example, wrote, 'The Antichrist...will reign three years and six months , and sit in the temple at Jerusalem' (*Against Heresies*, 30, 4. See also Commodianus, *Instructions*, 41). Augustine also spoke of a literal 42 month period (*City of God*, 20, 13). Many others since that time have adopted a similar understanding.

This is probably the most popular view in the evan-gelical-charismatic world today. The notes in the *Scofield Reference Bible* have been very influential in this regard. And best-sellers like Hal Lindsey's *Late, Great Planet Earth* have popularised this literal approach.

Also, the final seven years of Daniel's prophecy are

often related to the reign of the Antichrist. 'He will confirm a covenant with many for one seven,' writes Daniel. 'In the middle of the seven he will put an end to sacrifice and offering. And on a wing of the temple he will set up an abomination that causes desolation...' (Daniel 9:27). As the years of Daniel 9 are evidently literal years, so the years of Revelation are taken in the same way.

On the other hand, some other interpreters see the first part of this passage, as referring, not to the Antichrist, but to the Christ, Who put an end to the temple sacrifices by His death on the cross. (This is discussed in more detail in the section on the temple.)

Remember, however, that Revelation is a book of symbols. This time frame is symbolical. In the light of this, it has been suggested that this three and a half year period is intended to remind us of other periods in history when there were similar circumstances. For instance, the time of Antiochus Epiphanes who ruled over Judea in the second century before Christ (Swete, 1907; Morris, 1983, p.147).

The name 'Epiphanes' meant 'God is manifest' but the enemies of Antiochus called him 'Epimanes' which meant madman! He ruled over Palestine from 175 to 164 BC. Just over three years before his death, he initiated a time of terror and destruction for the Jews. He stormed Jerusalem, killing thousands and selling thousands more into slavery. He entered the Holy of Holies in the Temple and carried off many of the silver and gold vessels. Again, in 167 BC, he invaded the city on the Sabbath, slaughtered many people and issued decrees that the Jewish people had to stop living according to their laws and traditions. He erected a pagan altar over the altar of burnt offering in the Temple.

All of this sparked off the heroic Maccabean rebellion which in 164 BC resulted in the cleansing of the Temple. This was still fairly fresh in the minds of people of John's time - indeed, it is a period still remembered with both revulsion and pride by Jews today who celebrate its memory around Christmas time with the Feast of Lights.

In a sense, Antiochus serves as a model for the Antichrist. He tried to overrule the temple of God and to seek universal obeisance. Perhaps John was using this time period of approximately three and half years as a parallel for the reign of the Beast.

A more likely explanation seems to be the fairly obvious comparison between the era of the Antichrist and the rule of one of ancient Israel's most infamous kings - namely Ahab (Henriksen, 1940, 1986, p.143). According to James (5:17) there was a period of three and half years when there was no rain because of the word of Elijah. This was also a period of tyranny for the people of God. At queen Jezebel's instigation, prophets were put to death; many others were in hiding; and there was severe famine (1 Kings 18:1ff).

Yet it was also a time of miraculous provision for the people of God (1 Kings 17:1ff), and concluded with a dramatic triumph over the forces of evil at the confrontation between the prophets of Yahweh and the prophets of Baal on Mount Carmel (1 Kings 18:16ff).

Furthermore, the incidents described in Revelation 11:1-6 draw an obvious parallel between the days of Elijah and the days of the Antichrist. Here are two witnesses, who have power to shut the skies for a period of 42 months, just as Elijah did.

This is not to say that the time of the Antichrist will be of the same duration. The period is purely symbolic. Because of this, it cannot be taken literally. The reason for specifying 42 months is evidently to give us a clue that we are to look for other similar episodes in history to encourage us for such a time as this. In both the days of Antiochus and Ahab, the final victory was in the hands of the people of God! And so it will be in the time of the Antichrist.

John's vision of the Beast goes on to tell how he blasphemes the name of God and is given power to subdue the people of God. Finally, all the inhabitants of the earth worship him. No wonder this calls for 'patient endurance and faithfulness on the part of the saints'! It is a trying time!

It is also interesting to note that this time period of 42 months covers several other events as well. Firstly, it is the period during which the Holy City is trodden down by the Gentiles (11:2). Next, it is the period of the two witnesses (11:3), who probably represent the two fold ministry of regeneration and enduement with power (see Revelation 11:4 and Zechariah chapters 3 and 4). It is also the time during which the woman (who represents the people of God) is protected by God in the desert (12:14).

As all of these are contemporaneous, this helps us to understand what the number-symbols mean. Again, many people still take the numbers literally and thus are expecting all these things to occur in a concentrated fragment of history at the end of the age.

However, it seems evident that all of the passages listed actually refer to the whole church age! For instance, Jesus spoke of the 'times of the Gentiles' commencing at the fall of Jerusalem in AD 70 and continuing until the parousia (Luke 21:24ff). This seems to be the same length of time that John refers to when he describes the trampling of the Holy City (11:2) - yet he measures it as 42 months.

Next, the imagery of the two witnesses, who are described as two olive trees and two lampstands, suggests the whole gospel age. The picture is clearly taken from Zechariah chapters three and four, where we are told that it signifies the priest Joshua and the prince Zerubbabel. Joshua clearly represents the believer being cleansed and commissioned for priesthood and Zerubbabel equally clearly signifes the Spirit-filled life ('Not by might ... but by my Spirit', 4:6).

So the two witnesses of Revelation seem to suggest the age-long ongoing ministry of first of all, regeneration by the Spirit and secondly, impartation of power, by the same Spirit.

Thirdly, the Church has, in a sense, been wandering in the wilderness on its journey to the heavenly Canaan ever since its birth. So the description of the woman in the wilderness is a picture of this. It is interesting in this regard that there were 42 stopping places for the people of Israel when they journeyed from Egypt to the Promised Land (Numbers 33:5ff; see Morris, 1983, p.147). Is this also suggested by the 42 months?

In his description of the Antichrist, John goes on to introduce another figure. This is also a Beast, but this time from the land, not the sea. Elsewhere, he is called the False Prophet (19:20). The role of this False Prophet is to promote the cause of the Beast. So he performs miracles and signs, in order to draw people's allegiance (13:13ff). He makes an image for people to worship (13:14). He even gives life to the image! (13:15).

We can only speculate what all of this means. But if we take our clue from the idea that everything is symbolic, then once again, we realise that the image cannot actually be a material image - it must represent something else. Is it simply a way of saying that the Beast is presented in such a plausible way that people accept even the most preposterous behaviour? 'Marketing' is a modern term, but in every generation, tyrants have had those who have 'marketed' their philosophy and conduct in such a way that people have been willing to live and die for them. There are plenty of examples in the modern world - especially in some Middle Eastern countries.

Now follow two of the most oft-quoted identifying characteristics of John's description. First of all, everyone receives a mark on the right hand or the forehead -

> He also forced everyone, small and great, rich and poor, free and slave, to receive a mark on his right hand or on his forehead, so that no one could buy or sell unless he had the mark, which is the name of the beast or the number of his name (13:16,17).

Naturally, those who take the three and half years literally also take this passage literally. So there have been many stories about how this will actually be done. Some have argued that the credit card system will ultimately be replaced by a secret stamp on the hand or head. Others believe that governments will use such a mark to maintain control over what people do.

There was a story circulated in the US some years ago of someone who received a cheque from the Internal Revenue Service which they could not cash, because it had special instructions on it that it could only be cashed by identification through a code marking on the hand of the person concerned. This cheque was reputedly issued 'in error' and the affair hastily covered up.

Years later the IRS had received over one million letters from people protesting about this. The fact was that the incident never occurred in the first place.

Similarly, a Swedish bank journal issued a short report in the mid-1980's of the introduction of a credit system based on physical markings to the hand. Again, many Christians became variously alarmed and excited about this - alarmed because they did not approve, and excited because they saw it as a sign of the emergence of the Antichrist.

In fact, the report had been printed as a practical joke.

Of course, governments are very capable of such things. It could well happen. But whether this is a fulfilment of what John is talking about is another matter.

I suggest that the right hand signifies meaningful employment and that the forehead typifies freedom of thought. What the False Prophet is endeavouring to do is to control people's working lives and their thought lives. If they do not submit their talents and ideas to the Beast, they will be forbidden to buy or sell.

Once again, there are plenty of contemporary examples of this. How many political prisoners languish in jails around the world because they utterly refuse to work for a corrupt or tyrannical government, or to allow their thinking to be controlled by a totalitarian power. Christians, in particular, suffer in this way. And they have done so from the circuses of Rome to the gulags of Russia.

Or, if not imprisoned, many such people simply cannot get jobs. A few years ago, my wife and I visited a church in a Middle Eastern country where the pianist was a very talented engineer, frequently bypassed in his profession because of his Christian faith. He was fortunate. In that same country, not long afterwards, other believers were imprisoned without trial.

The other very popular aspect of John's description of the Antichrist is his number -

This calls for wisdom. If anyone has insight, let him calculate the number of the beast, for it is man's number.

His number is 666.

(Revelation 13:18)

What speculation this has caused! In Australia, when a national credit card called Bankcard was released, it had the letter 'b' in three colours. It looked something like a triple six. Many people saw it is a sign of the Antichrist.

In Jerusalem, taxis have numbers beginning '666'. I have heard of Christians who refuse to ride in them!

Many expect that during the reign of the Antichrist, people will actually have this number stamped on them.

Again, however, let us remind ourselves that what we have here is symbolism - a message in code. Just as we cannot take the description of the Beast with seven heads and ten horns literally, so we ought not to take this literally. If we see one part of the chapter as figurative we should take it all the same way.

So what does it mean? A very old and esteemed idea is that it somehow refers to the Roman Empire. (Which, by the way, was a good reason to have it in 'code'. A more direct statement would have been very dangerous.)

Irenaeus for example, offers several interesting suggestions (*Against Heresies,* c.185 AD, 30, 3). Using the fact that in the Greek alphabet, letters doubled as numbers, he considers, first of all, the word Lateinos. If you add up the letter values of this name, it comes out as follows -

L	=	30
A	=	1
T	=	300
E	=	5
I	=	10

N	= 50
O	= 70
S	= 200

$$666$$

Irenaeus sees this as representing the Roman Empire, which he points out, was also the fourth kingdom mentioned by Daniel.

He goes on to suggest that the name Teitan is another possibility. This adds up in a similar fashion to 666; it has six letters; it is not the actual name of any particular king; it was an ascription used for the sun-god; and was once the name of a tyrant.

However, Irenaeus is wise enough to say that he 'will not incur the risk of pronouncing positively as to the name of the Antichrist'.

In more recent times, others have gone back to the name 'Lateinos' and suggested that it refers to the papacy (eg Foster, p.70).

On the other hand, it has been argued that the number refers to Nero. To achieve this, however, it is necessary to take the words 'Nero Caesar' and then to transliterate them to Hebrew! (Moffatt, ENT, 1967, p.434).

As we have mentioned before, there have been attempts to take names like Hitler and Stalin and to make them fit as well.

The simplest solution seems again to be the obvious one. Numbers often have a symbolic value in Scripture. The number seven, for example, is frequently symbolic of God. The book of Revelation itself abounds in examples. The Holy Spirit is depicted as seven spirits (1:4; 3:1; 5:6); there are seven letters to seven churches (2:1ff); there are seven seals (5:1), seven angels (8:2), seven trumpets (8:6), seven thunders (10:3), seven plagues (15:1) and seven golden bowls (15:7).

The number three is also important. So there are three persons in the Godhead. There are three gates on each side of the Holy City (Revelation 21:13ff). David chose three mighty men (2 Samuel 23:8). Jesus was three days in the grave. And so on.

So when we combine three and seven we have 777. So what is the number 666? Is it not simply a human attempt to duplicate that divine number - but one that falls short every time? Man is always only a six - never a seven.

THE NUMBER OF THE BEAST

| 777 | = | DIVINE PERFECTION |

| 666 | = | HUMAN IMPERFECTION |

'It is man's number' (Rev. 13:18)

It is quite valid, in fact, to translate the relevant phrase in Revelation 13:18 simply as 'man's number' (as in the New International Version). In other words, it is not necessarily the number of a particular man, but rather of man in general.

So when we try to identify the Antichrist, we may be making a mistake if we look only for one individual. May we not be wiser to identify the spirit of Antichrist wherever it occurs?

It is interesting to note also that there is a combination in Revelation 13 between political and religious power. The Beast is a political figure; the False Prophet is a religious one.

Such a combination is the most dangerous ever known to man. When religion is given secular clout, it can be terrifying. The Medieval Church is an example. It is no wonder the Reformers saw it as Antichristian!

On Christmas Day, AD 800, while Charlemagne of the Franks was worshipping in Rome, the pope placed a crown on his head and called him Holy Roman Emperor. Charlemagne made the mistake of accepting this. In doing so, he acknowledged the pope's right to make kings - which, inevitably, meant the right to unmake them as well. What resulted, as Voltaire once wrote, was neither holy, nor Roman, nor indeed, an empire. So began centuries of darkness for both Church and State.

The Church owned one third of all the real estate in Europe. It forcibly extracted money from people who could often ill afford it. It ruled over rulers and made kingdoms subject to it. It could enthrone or dethrone emperors. It could determine the destiny of nations. The Spanish Inquisition has become a symbol of the lowest depths of this period. In all of its history, no accused person was ever acquitted; most people were tortured; many lost their lives; many were banished or exiled.

It was only the Reformation that initiated the required change.

In more recent times, we have seen the blending of Islam with politics. Among other tragic results of this was the appalling loss of life in the Iran-Iraq war - over 1 million casualties by the end of 1986.

I must confess to some sense of alarm when I hear of Christians advocating political action. The weapons of our warfare are not carnal and we do well to remember that. One problem with religion is that dedicated believers are usually people of such conviction that they are sure they are right. If they are wrong, however, but do not recognise it, they can cause great harm. This is exacerbated if they have political means at their disposal to enforce their will. There are many examples from history of great harm being done in the name of God, by people who thought they were His servants, but in reality, were not. It is virtually impossible to change the minds of such people. They are convinced they are right. By contrast, people who govern through reason and persuasion are open to mellowing and to change. Where those of misguided religious conviction have no material or political power at their disposal, they cannot do a great deal of harm; when the reverse is the case, the harm can be incalculable.

The early Church transformed the world by the preaching of the gospel. It was only in the fourth century, when Constantine became the first Christian emperor, that political strength became theirs. It has often been argued that this was the beginning of a decline in true Christianity, from which we still have not fully recovered. Indeed, it may well be that had Christians simply continued to proclaim the gospel of Christ in simplicity and love, we would live in a much different world today!

In summary, it is interesting to see how in so many ways, the Antichrist is an imitation of the Christ. The chart at the end of this section lists in summary form a number of parallels between the two. It is worth looking at closely for it really highlights the essential nature of Antichrist. He is not so much an individual as a spiritual force.

The point seems to me to be this. What John is describing is the kind of thing that can, in fact, happen in any age. Was Nero the Beast? Was the medieval papacy? Was Hitler? Was Stalin? Was the Ayatollah Khomeini? The answer to all these questions is both yes and no. None of them were, yet all of them were! In other words, no single person is alone the Antichrist. As John wrote, there are plenty of antichrists all the time. Yet on the other hand, each of them was the Antichrist for his era!

No doubt there will be one major Antichrist figure at the end of the age. Paul, in particular, seems to suggest this in 2 Thessalonians. But meanwhile, there is always the possibility of an Antichrist anywhere in the world at any time.

This is the genius of the Book of Revelation. This is why it is always relevant. Believers of every age can read it and see how it applies to them. Saints in the days of persecuting emperors like Domitian and Marcus Aurelius, could read it and find comfort in it. Simple believers in the days of the Spanish Inquisition could be encouraged by it. Followers of Christ in China or Iran today can find a message there for them.

A friend once said to me, 'The facts are not as important as the truth'. If we apply that to Revelation, we can see that even if we make a mistake about interpreting it, we can still be blessed by the truth of it. Of course, we should do all we can to be careful and accurate in our study. But even if we fail to grasp all the details, or actually get them wrong, the message is still there for all to read.

And what is the message? Simply that the Antichrist may do all he likes, but ultimately the true Christ will triumph. So the last reference we have to the Beast is -

I saw heaven standing open and there before me was a white horse, whose rider is called Faithful and True. With justice he judges and makes war. His eyes are like blazing fire, and on his head are many crowns. He has a name written on him that no one knows but he himself. He is dressed in a robe dipped in blood, and his name is the Word of God.

The armies of heaven were following him, riding on white horses and dressed in fine linen, white and clean. Out of his mouth comes a sharp sword with which to strike down the nations...

On his robe and on his thigh he has this name written: KING OF KINGS AND LORD OF LORDS.

Then I saw the beast and the kings of the earth and their armies gathered together to make war against the rider on the horse and his army. But the beast was captured, and with him the false prophet ... The two of them were thrown alive into the fiery lake of burning sulphur.

(Revelation 19:11-20)

Christ and Antichrist Contrasted and Compared

The simplest way to interpret the symbols used about the Antichrist is to take the clue given in 2 Thessalonians 2:4, that he proclaims himself to be God. Everything about him is a reflection or reversal of the true Christ. So we can compare and contrast the features of each. By so doing we avoid the often fruitless quest of trying to identify each feature of the Antichrist with a specific event or date.

Note: Please read 2 Thessalonians 2:1-17; 1 John 2:18-21 and Revelation Chapters 11, 12, 13, 17 and 19 before examining this chart.

CHRIST	ANTICHRIST
1. Christ is the second Person of the Holy Trinity - Father, Son and Holy Spirit (2 Cor 13:14; Matt 28:19).	1. The Antichrist is the second person of an unholy trilogy - the Dragon, the Beast and the False Prophet (Rev 12:3; 13:1; 13:11; 19:20; 20:2).
2. Christ is the ever-living One, the Alpha and the Omega, who was	2. The Antichrist is the one 'who once was, now is not, and yet will come' (Rev

CHRIST	ANTICHRIST
and is and is to come (Rev 1:4,8,17f; 2:8; 22:13).	17:8).
3. Christ came to earth from heaven (John 6:38; Phil 2:6ff).	3. The Antichrist comes from the Abyss (Rev 11:7).
4. Christ is divine (John 1:1ff; Phil 2:11).	4. The Antichrist claims to be divine (2 Thess 2:4).
5. Christ is worthy of worship and honour (Rev 5:12-14).	5. The Antichrist claims worship (2 Thess 2:4; Rev 13:8).
6. Christ is the image of God (Col 1:15; Heb 1:3).	6. The Antichrist is the image of Satan (Rev 12:3; 13:1).
7. Christ is the Holy One of God (Mark 1:24).	7. The Antichrist is the lawless one (2 Thess 2:8).
8. Christ is the embodiment of truth (John 14:6).	8. The Antichrist is a liar (2 Thess 2:9,11).
9. Christ worked miracles by the power of the Holy Spirit, culminating in His	9. The Antichrist performs miracles by the power of the False Prophet (2

CHRIST	ANTICHRIST
resurrection (John 20:30,31; Luke 4:18; Acts 10:38; Romans 1:4).	Thess 2:9; Rev 13:13-15).
10. The Holy Spirit testifies to Him (John 16:13-15; Rev 2:7,11,17,29; 3:6, 13, 22).	10. The False Prophet testifies to him (Rev 13:11; 19:20).
11. The number 'seven' used of Him equals perfection (Rev 1:12,16,20; 5:6; 6:1, etc.).	11. The numbers '6' and '3½' used of him indicate imperfection (Rev 12:14; 13:5,18). e.g. '3½' is half of 7 and '666' shows how man always falls short of God's perfection.
12. Christ's ministry on earth lasted 3½ years.	12. The Antichrist's time period (3½ years = 42 months = 1260 days) is a copy of this (Rev 11:11; 12:14; 13:5).
13. Christ reigns from a position of permanent and total authority (Matt 28:19;	13. The Antichrist has a temporary authority (Rev 13:7; 19:20).

CHRIST	ANTICHRIST
Eph 1:19b-23; 1 Cor 15:25).	
14. Christ is a lamb and a lion (Rev 5:5,6), i.e. a blend of meekness and majesty.	14. The Antichrist is a leopard, a bear and a lion (Rev 13:2), i.e. a blend of aggression and ferocity.
15. Christ died, but rose again (Rev 1:8; 5:6).	15. The Antichrist receives a deadly wound but is healed (Rev 13:3,4).
16. Christ demands total allegiance from His followers (Luke 14:26ff).	16. The Antichrist imposes allegiance on his followers (Rev 13:17).
17. Christ leads His followers to life (John 3:36).	17. The Antichrist leads his followers to death (2 Thess 2:12; Rev 20:15).
18. Christ has one head, but many crowns (Rev 19:12).	18. The Antichrist has seven heads but still only ten crowns (Rev 13:1).
19. Christ is exalted to heaven (Phil 2:9).	19. The Antichrist is consigned to hell (Rev 19:20).

7. Will the Jewish temple be rebuilt?

Some years ago, my wife and I were in Israel with a group of Australian Christians.

We were gathered with thousands of believers from around the world one Sunday morning for a special march of witness and a prayer service at the Western Wall. It was an exciting occasion.

There were Jewish people praying at the Wall, the men on the left and the women on the right. Many of the men were clothed in traditional black suits and black hats, with prayer shawls. Some had phylacteries strapped around their arms or foreheads. Some prayed in groups; others alone, often standing close to the wall and rocking back and forth as they intoned their petitions. Little pieces of paper were jammed between the huge stones, each one containing a prayer.

Above them could be seen the golden orb of the Mosque of Omar, or as it is otherwise known, the Dome of the Rock. Here was a Moslem shrine towering over a Jewish holy place. And not far away was a group of a few thousand Christians praying to their Messiah! The Christians had marched from the Mount of Olives singing songs of praise and celebrating the resurrection on that Lord's Day morning. There had been smiles, laughter, dancing and joy as we rejoiced together. People had leaned out of buses waving to us, as they saw the signs proclaiming a love for Israel. When Arab buses passed, however, there was a reserved silence.

Not everyone was pleased. One Israeli, trying to steer his wife and children through the Christian crowd, became very angry at the obstruction we caused and shouted at us angrily to go away.

But all in all it was an inspiring time of celebration.

At the Wall, the leader of the rally invited us to join in prayer for Israel. Then he suggested we repeat a prayer after him. He began with expressions of worship which we were glad to follow. Next he began to ask God to bless the people of Israel. Again, we were happy to join in.

But then he began to pray for the rebuilding of the Jewish temple. At that point, I bailed out! That was one prayer I felt I couldn't pray. But almost everyone else, it seemed, continued. Who was right?

First of all, it might be helpful to consider the Jewish perspective. Naturally, we might think, they would like to have the temple rebuilt. In fact, this is not necessarily the case. Many Jews are not really interested. Their viewpoint was summarised to me by Mrs Fran Alpert, a Jewish archaelologist -

'For a start, a temple would need a high priest. However, we have no way of knowing today who that should be. The records have long since been lost. Secondly, a temple would need a sacrificial system. Most Jewish people today believe that prayer and devotion have replaced the sacrificial system - as the later prophets said, God desires mercy, not sacrifice. Thirdly, we don't know the exact spot on which the temple should stand.'

This latter question, of course, is of no little interest. If the Dome of the Rock stands on the actual temple site, then it would be necessary for the mosque to be demolished before the temple could be built! It is not hard to imagine the ramifications of this. The Dome of the Rock is the third most sacred edifice in Islam. In fact, one simple way to enrage - and unite - the Islamic nations would be to blow it up!

One Israeli once told a friend of mine that the Jews would not actually destroy the mosque, but that they were praying for an earthquake! Even so, the likelihood of Moslems agreeing to a temple being built there is very slim, to say the least.

On the other hand, there is some debate about the exact temple site. Professor Kauffmann of the Hebrew University has written a paper in which he argues that the temple stood on an area of cleared ground just to the north of the Dome of the Rock.

If he is right, then the temple could actually be built there without the mosque being touched.

However, in reality, the two buildings would be so close that such an arrangement would be quite unworkable.

In simple terms, there are major practical objections to the erection of a new temple on Mount Moriah. Of course, this is not necessarily a reason why it should not be built. There are numerous examples from history of God doing things that are humanly or physically impossible. And Lindsey, for example, seems to see no problem. Sure, it will cause some upset to the Arab world, but so what? (Lindsey, 1974, p.140f). But nevertheless, all the factors do need to be considered.

What about the biblical position? First of all, those who believe that the temple will be rebuilt obviously have Scriptural reasons for this concept. Indeed, the idea is a very old one. In the late second century, Irenaeus, for instance, wrote that the Antichrist would 'sit in the temple at Jerusalem' (*Against Heresies,* 30,4). Other writers have taken up a similar view over the centuries (eg Stanton, p.130) - although the opinion is not as widespread as might be expected, especially among scholars.

Firstly, it is based on Paul's words in 2 Thessalonians that the man of lawlessness will set himself up 'in God's temple, proclaiming himself to be God' (2.4). This picture is confirmed by the frequent repetition in Revelation 13 of the idea of the Beast being worshipped. Obviously, if the Antichrist is to sit in the temple, there must be a temple for him to occupy.

Furthermore, there are several references in the Old Testament to Levites and to sacrifices being offered in the age to come. So in Isaiah we read -

> All nations will come and see my glory ... And they will bring all your brothers, from all the nations, to my holy mountain in Jerusalem as an offering to the Lord ... They will bring them, as the Israelites bring their grain offerings to the temple of the Lord ... And I will select some of them also to be priests and Levites, says the Lord.
>
> (Isaiah 66:18ff)

Similarly, Jeremiah claims that there will always be a priest to offer burnt offerings (Jeremiah 33:18) and Ezekiel says that the Lord will put His sanctuary (temple) among His people forever (37:26).

Thirdly, there is the lengthy passage in Ezekiel describing a huge rebuilt temple. The picture involves nine chapters (40 - 48 inclusive) and goes into fine detail. So far, this building has never been erected - could it be that it is still to come?

Next, Daniel talks about the Antichrist making a covenant for seven years in the middle of which he will put an end to sacrifice and offering (Daniel 9:27). If this is so, 'the Israelis will then be permitted to re-instate the sacrifice and offering aspect of the law of Moses' (Lindsey, 1974, p.140).

Furthermore, Daniel goes on to say that he will set up the abomination that causes desolation 'on a wing of the temple'. All of this demands that the temple be rebuilt. According to the law of Moses, 'sacrifices can be offered only in the temple at Jerusalem' and obviously, the reference to 'a wing of the temple' demands a temple!

Finally, the Mount of Olives discourse by Christ clearly centres the great tribulation on Jerusalem. He also refers to the abomination that causes desolation standing in the holy place, which obviously implies a temple (Matthew 24:15).

To take the last passage first, I have already suggested that Jesus was actually talking about the fall of Jerusalem in AD 70 when He gave these predictions (see above on the tribulation). And further on, we shall look at the suggestion that prophecies concerning Israel are often fulfilled in the Church. If these points are correct, there is no need for a temple to be rebuilt.

Regarding the prophecies of Daniel, there is considerable debate about who it is who makes the covenant. This is what Daniel actually says -

> Know and understand this: from the issuing of the decree to rebuild Jerusalem until the Anointed One, the ruler, comes, there shall be seven 'sevens' and sixty-two 'sevens' ...
> After the sixty-two sevens, the Anointed One will be cut off and will have nothing. The people of the ruler who will come will destroy the city and the sanctuary. The end will come like a flood. War will continue till the end, and desolations have been decreed. He will confirm a covenant with many for one 'seven'. In the middle of the 'seven' he will put an end to sacrifice and offering. And on a wing of the temple he will set up an abomination that causes desolation, until the end that is decreed is poured out on him.

(Daniel 9:25ff)

It would be very tempting to go into a detailed study of this passage and its context. However, I shall have to resist the temptation! The real question is simply whether this is in fact a prophecy about Antichrist.

First of all, both historicists and futurists usually agree that the 'seven sevens' and '62 sevens' are 69 weeks of years, that is, 483 years. There are various starting points suggested for this period, but using Nehemiah 2:1-8, we can suggest BC 445 as the year of the decree to rebuild Jerusalem. This takes us to about AD 30. At this time, the Anointed One, the Lord Jesus Christ, is cut off. So far, no problem. From here on, however, there are serious differences.

Futurists usually now argue that there is a huge gap between the 69th week and the 70th week, and that the last week is the final seven years of the age (Pentecost, 1981, pp.246ff). Hence, the 'ruler who will come' (v.26) is the Antichrist, who destroys the city. Similarly, the word 'he' at the beginning of verse 27 refers to the Antichrist who will make a covenant with the Jews, will put an end to the temple sacrifices and will set up an abomination in the temple.

That verses 26 and 27 refer to the Antichrist is view shared by commentators from other schools of thought as well, even if they don't hold a dispensationalist approach.

There is a real problem, however, with slipping thousands of years in between the numbers 69 and 70! On what authority do we do this?

Historicists, therefore, argue that the 'ruler who will come' is actually Titus, who destroyed Jerusalem in AD 70, and that the 'He' of verse 27 is Christ.

Let's look at this latter point. It is really quite difficult to know just who is the subject of verse 27. Grammatically, it could refer back to either the Anointed One (the Messiah) of verse 25 or the 'ruler' of verse 26. That it refers to the Messiah is consistent with the fact that He is the subject of the previous verse. And He certainly did 'confirm a covenant with many' and by His death there came an end to temple sacrifices. The translation of the last part of verse 27 is not clear enough for us to be dogmatic about who is responsible for the actions mentioned there (Hall, 1969, pp.545 ff).

In summary, we have to say that there are so many questions about this passage, that it would be very unwise to be too dogmatic in any direction. However, it is very clear that the first part, at least, is a remarkable prophecy about the first advent of our Lord Jesus Christ. And there do seem to be problems with postponing the seventieth week to the end of the age.

To use the passage as evidence for a rebuilt temple prior to the parousia is dubious, to say the least.

And one other point needs mentioning here, too. Some writers talk of the temple being rebuilt, of the sacrificial system being reinstituted and then stopped again, all within the space of three and a half years (eg Lindsey, 1974, pp.140f). For an edifice so significant as the temple, it seems highly unlikely that such a project would be undertaken hastily. Great care would be devoted to planning, designing and so on. This would be more likely to be a process of decades rather than years!

Now, what about Ezekiel's vision? There are some practical difficulties with it. The major one is that according to the dimensions given, it would be physically impossible to build the temple which Ezekiel describes! According to one commentator, the building itself would cover an area as large as the whole area of the Old City of Jerusalem and the courtyards would require land six times that occupied by modern London! (J. Sidlow Baxter, 1952, p.32).

Furthermore, the river Jordan would need to be moved to one side to make room and Jerusalem itself would need to be relocated.

It seems plain that Ezekiel's vision is just that - a

vision, not intended to be taken literally. Like the New Jerusalem described in Revelation 21, which is obviously depicted figuratively (it is cube-shaped, for a start!) what Ezekiel describes is also a magnificent pageant of the glory of God when His kingdom is established. It represents the Church in this present age and the everlasting realm of heaven in the age to come.

The other Old Testament passages must be interpreted similarly. It is true that there will always be a priest for the people of God, and that there will always be a sanctuary. But the name of the High Priest is Jesus and all of God's people are now priests with Him. So when Jeremiah prophesies that there will never cease to be a priest ministering before the Lord, it is in Jesus and His Church that this is fulfilled. There can be no doubt about this, as the New Testament makes it very plain.

First of all, it teaches that every believer is now a priest (1 Peter 2:5,9; Revelation 1:6). In fact, what this means is that God's original intention is restored, for from the beginning, His purpose was that all of His people should be priests (Exodus 19:6). The choice of the Levitical tribe to represent the nation was a modification provided later (Numbers 3:5ff). In simple terms, this now means that no one needs to use an intermediary in order to pray, seek forgiveness, or to make an offering because every believer has access to the throne of God at any time.

This is possible because we now also have a great High Priest, and through Him we can come confidently before God -

Therefore, since we have a great high priest who has gone through the heavens, Jesus the Son of God, let us hold firmly to the faith we profess. For we do not have a high priest who is unable to

187

sympathise with our weaknesses, but we have one who has been tempted in every way, just as we are - yet was without sin. Let us then approach the throne of grace with confidence, so that we may receive mercy and find grace to help us in our time of need.

(Hebrews 4:14-16)

So there is no basis whatever for assuming that Old Testament prophecies about a continuing priesthood will be fulfilled in an earthly temple in modern Israel. It is in the Church that they find their expression. The sanctuary of God is now the people of God.

What about what Paul says in his second letter to the Thessalonians, when he describes the Antichrist as setting himself up in God's temple (2:4)? It is interesting to note his use of words. There are two Greek nouns that can both be translated as 'temple' in English. The first is *hieron*. This word is normally used in the New Testament for the actual physical building that stood in Jerusalem. An example of this occurs in Matthew 24, at the beginning of Jesus' talk to His disciples on the Mount of Olives about the destruction of the Holy City.

Jesus left the temple and was walking away when his disciples came up to him to call his attention to its buildings. 'Do you see all these things?' he asked. 'I tell you the truth, not one stone here will be left on another; every one will be thrown down.'

There can be no doubt that the Lord was making reference here to the literal, material, physical temple that stood proudly in His own day on the north-east corner of Jerusalem.

Similar uses of the word *hieron* occur in John 2:13 and Acts 3:1.

The other word is *naos*. This word is usually used in a metaphorical sense. For instance, when Jesus was

188

accused of being able to restore a demolished temple in three days, his detractors took Him literally. But Jesus was referring to His own body and used the word *naos*.

Furthermore, Paul frequently uses this noun in referring to the Church as a temple. He reminds the Corinthians, for example, that they are, as a church, the temple of God (1 Corinthians 3:16-17). Later, he points out that each individual believer is also a temple of the Holy Spirit (1 Corinthians 6:19,20) -

> Do you not know that your body is a temple of the Holy Spirit, who is in you, whom you have received from God? You are not your own; you were bought at a price. Therefore honour God with your body.

The emphasis here is obviously not on bricks and mortar, but on the human body - God's new dwelling place.

Similarly, to the Ephesians, Paul draws a multi-coloured picture of Jews and Gentiles together being built into a 'holy temple to the Lord' (2:21). The foundation is composed of apostles and prophets and Jesus Christ is Himself the chief cornerstone. The whole structure is designed to be a dwelling place for the Holy Spirit of God (2:22).

In all of these cases, the word used for 'temple' is not *hieron* but *naos*. It is interesting to note that Paul employs the same word in 2 Thessalonians 2:4. There can be little doubt that it is the Church to which the apostle is referring here. This man of lawlessness, this son of perdition, will actually establish himself in the very Church itself.

This is further made obvious by the phrase 'God's temple'. The Jewish temple was no longer the temple of God at the time Paul wrote. It had now been supplanted by the Church. It is inconceivable that the apostle would even suggest that the temple was God's dwelling place.

This is another reason why so many of the Reformers felt that the Antichrist was embodied in the papacy. Here was an institution whose head literally made claims to be God on earth. And he was seated right at the very heart of the 'temple'.

THE TEMPLE

HIERON
- Physical building (Matt. 24:1)
- Now destroyed (Matt. 24:2)

NAOS
- God's dwelling place (1 Cor. 3:16, 17)
- Still being built (Eph. 2:21)

The Church — the temple of God

For these reasons, I do not believe there is any biblical warrant for looking for a rebuilt Jewish temple. Even if there will be a period of just three and half years of Antichristian dominion at the end of the age, it will be centred in the Church, not in a Judaistic building. Personally, I see something even more sinister. I see the spirit of Antichrist being present throughout the whole gospel era - perhaps intensified at the very end - and infecting the Church over and over again. There can be no doubt that this has been the case with the papacy at times. But it has also been the case in other parts of the Church, too.

No area is immune. In charismatic and evangelical circles, the same thing can happen - indeed, Jesus specifically warned us of this when He told us that even some miracle-workers would be rejected by Him. In spite of their claims, He would not own them as any of His (Matthew 7:21ff).

There is a further aspect to this question of a rebuilt temple, too. Let's go back to the incident at the Western Wall, with which I began this section.

The main reason I found it impossible to go along with the prayer that the man in question was praying, actually had nothing to do with eschatology. My instinctive response was to shout out, 'How can we pray for the re-establishment of something that our Lord Jesus died to abolish? How can we seriously ask God to bless the reintroduction of a system that was phased out at the cross?'

Even if it were possible to prove from the Scriptures that a new temple should be erected in Jerusalem, we would still have no warrant to pray for it! The old covenant is obsolete, says the writer to the Hebrews (8:13). We now have a High Priest Who has a permanent priesthood (Hebrews 7:24) and Who made a sacrifice that dealt with sin 'once for all' (Hebrews 7:27).

To pray for any other system to be introduced is tantamount to blasphemy. It is certainly a denial of the efficacy of the blood of Christ. I have no doubt that the prayer leader at the Wall had not thought this through - in fact I know him to be a genuine believer in the Lord Jesus. Nevertheless, he ought not to have prayed as he did.

It is my belief, then, that there is no biblical warrant for believing that there should be or will be another temple on Mount Moriah. In fact, we can go even further and say that even if such a temple were rebuilt it would not be a fulfilment of biblical prophecy.

The purposes of God are now being realised in His new sanctuary, His people, who, as Paul explains so well, are being 'built together to become a dwelling place in which God lives by his Spirit' (Ephesians 2:22).

8. What is the role of Israel in God's purposes today?

In the previous section, I mentioned an occasion when my wife, Vanessa, and I were at a rally near the Western Wall in Jerusalem, and a prayer was offered for the rebuilding of the temple.

Part of the reason why that prayer was prayed, lay in the fact that the man concerned had a very high view of the role of Israel as a nation. He was convinced that Israel would be central to the plans of God for the destiny of mankind.

In fact, I spoke with him later and he said to me, 'Don't you believe that Jerusalem should be a Jewish city and that it will eventually be the capital of the world?'

In a book of this size, it is not possible to go into this question in detail. The subject demands a volume in its own right! So all we can do is look at a couple of representative passages.

Before we do so, however, it may be helpful to define just what we mean by the term 'Israel'. Actually, it has several different meanings in the Bible. Originally, it was the name given to Jacob after God chose him to be the father of a new nation. Jacob had wrestled with an angel for a whole night (Genesis 32:22ff) and as a result was renamed Israel (32:28) which means 'he struggles with God'.

As Jacob had twelve sons and each of them became the progenitor of a clan or tribe, these twelve tribes collectively became known as the tribes of Israel (Exodus 1:1ff). It was quite common practice in Bible days for a nation to be named after its founder, and even to be spoken of in the singular, as if the nation itself were still one person (eg Exodus 17:8-11; Numbers 21:1ff).

In the tenth century before Christ, Israel split into two parts. The southern part took the name Judah, after its most dominant tribe; but the northern part retained the name Israel. Thus, Israel then came to mean only the northern section of the original kingdom (2 Samuel 5:4,5; 1 Kings 12:16ff; Amos 1:1).

It is important to realise this if we are to have a clear understanding of the many references to Israel from this time on. Sometimes the original nation may still be intended, but more often than not, it will be only the northern part. This grouping of tribes is commonly referred to as the 'Ten Tribes', and after the Assyrian exile, as the 'Ten Lost Tribes'. This is something of an oversimplification, because, when the division occurred, some members of all ten tribes migrated to the south so that they could maintain true temple worship (2 Chronicles 11:16). So not all of the ten tribes were deported. Nevertheless, it is broadly true.

Even more confusing, the northern kingdom was sometimes referred to as Ephraim, after its largest tribe, named after one of Joseph's two sons (Ezekiel 37:19ff; Hosea 5:3ff).

In the sixth century, the southern kingdom of Judah was invaded by the forces of Babylon and most of them were taken captive. When some of them returned in 536 BC they were called Jews (from the word for Judah). However, with the decimation of the northern kingdom, they also began to use the name of Israel! (Ezra 3:1; Ezekiel 3:4ff).

ISRAEL

- = Jacob. . . Gen. 35:9-10
- = Nation of 12 tribes. . . Ex. 1:1ff
- = Nation of 10 tribes. . . 2 Sam. 5:1ff; 1 Kings 12:16ff.
- = Nation of 2 tribes. . . Ezra 3:1; Ezek. 3:4ff
- = The Church. . . Rom. 9:6; Gal. 6:16

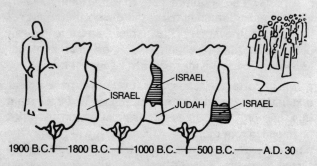

1900 B.C.—1800 B.C.—1000 B.C.—500 B.C.——A.D. 30

So when we talk about Israel, we need to know which Israel we mean! Is it the original nation, or the northern part only? The southern part only, or some or all of these?

By New Testament times, it usually meant the remnant of the southern kingdom that remained from the Babylonian Exile. This meant the tribe of Judah in particular, but included members of all tribes (compare Luke 2:36). In other words, the Jews.

194

So what is the role of Israel today? First of all, we need to look at the well-known prophecy of Ezekiel. Among other things, he prophesies that God will bring the Israelites back to their own land and that the people of both the northern kingdom of Israel and the southern kingdom of Judah will be reunited as one nation -

> I will take the Israelites out of the nations where they have gone. I will gather them from all around and bring them back into their own land. I will make them one nation in the land, on the mountains of Israel.
>
> (37:21,22)

Similarly, Isaiah declares -

> In that day, the Lord will reach out his hand a second time to reclaim the remnant that is left of his people from Assyria, from Lower Egypt, from Cush, from Elam, from Babylonia, from Hamath and from the islands of the sea.
>
> (Isaiah 11:11)

Both of these passages are popularly seen as being fulfilled in the years since World War 2, when hundreds of thousands of Jews flocked back into the Holy Land to re-establish the nation of Israel. So spectacular has been the rise of this small, isolated, militant nation, and so dramatic have been its victories in war and in peace, that Christians everywhere have excitedly proclaimed the whole phenomenon as a fulfilment of prophecy.

The Israelis themselves have been quick to quote Old Testament Scriptures to illustrate what they are doing - the desert, for instance, has indeed blossomed like a rose under their care and industry (Isaiah 35:1).

However, some caution is needed here. First of all, Ezekiel was an exile in Babylon when he wrote his prophecy. For him, the return of the people of God to the land of Israel was still future. When they did go back in 536 BC, was this a fulfilment of his prophecy, even then?

Similarly, Isaiah's reference to the Lord gathering His people 'a second time' is a reference to the exodus from Egypt. This was the first time He rescued His people from the oppression of foreigners. The return from Babylon was the second time.

In a literal sense, then, there is no need for there to be a further fulfilment of these prophecies. This is not to say that there cannot be a further application. As I have mentioned already, this is the divine genius of prophecy - it can be shown to be relevant over and over again. But it is to express caution about too ready a claim that the prophecy is being fulfilled in our day - and only in our day.

Thirdly, part of the promise of restoration is that Israel would be renewed spiritually.

> I will sprinkle clean water on you, and you will be clean; I will cleanse you from all your impurities and from all your idols. I will give you a new heart and put a new spirit in you; I will remove from you your heart of stone and give you a heart of flesh. And I will put my Spirit in you ... You will live in the land I gave your forefathers; you will be my people, and I will be your God.
>
> (Ezekiel 36:25ff)

In some respects, this was fulfilled after the Exile. Prior to this, idolatry had been a recurring problem in Israel. It never was again. Further, Christianity was born in the land as God did pour out His Spirit four centuries later.

Can it be said that this passage is being fulfilled in modern Israel?

There are very few Israelis who are believers in Jesus Christ, although the number is growing. Most believers are Arabs. These Arab Christians do not see the establishment of the State of Israel as a fulfilment of prophecy at all. 'The return of the Jews to this land has nothing to do with Christianity,' one Arab pastor told me. 'It is purely a political thing. It has caused bitterness and bloodshed and division. We cannot see Christ in that at all.'

This same man has testified that through the power of the gospel, he has learned to love the Jewish people and he has frequent fellowship with Messianic believers. So he bears no grudge and has no axe to grind. But he went on to say , 'Ezekiel not only talked about 'the return of Israel to the land, he also declared that they would be cleansed from their sinfulness and that they would return to God. Moreover, they would be ruled by 'David their prince' - surely a reference to Christ - and not by a secular government. The government in the land today is quite secular. There are many religious Jews, of course. Some are quite fanatical. But most Jews do not practise their religion seriously. Certainly, you could not call the government a spiritual one! It is as secular, political and military as any in the world.'

Comments like these must cause us to be cautious before jumping too rapidly to the conclusion that modern Israel is fulfilling Bible prophecy.

It seems more reasonable to see Ezekiel's predictions as having been fulfilled initially in the fifth century BC. On the other hand, there is also a spiritual dimension to them. May they not also be prophetically fulfilled in the Church? As a matter of interest, most Christians see them like this, in practice, anyway. We often take the passage about dry bones, for instance, and apply it to spiritual renewal today. Similarly, we use the verses about a new heart and a new spirit when considering new birth and so on. It is worth noting again how selective we can be in our use of Scripture! In cavalier fashion, we take one passage literally, another metaphorically and yet another in both ways! In many cases, of course, it doesn't really matter. But sometimes it does.

In fact, the New Testament actually gives us some guidelines about how to interpret the Old Testament. A parallel passage from Jeremiah 31, for example, is quoted by the writer to the Hebrews as applying to the new covenant in Christ (Jeremiah 31:31-34; Hebrews 8:8ff; 10:16). This gives us a precedent as to how we are supposed to understand such scriptures. It is clear that it is perfectly valid to apply them in a spiritual sense to the Church.

Furthermore, there are parts of Ezekiel's prophecy which simply cannot be applied literally. The reference to Israel taking seven months to bury their dead (39:12) is a case in point. One writer has estimated that this would involve 360 million corpses! (Grier, 1970, p.36). Not to mention the enormous problems of pestilence and corruption. Obviously, we are not supposed to take this literally. The number 'seven' is evidently symbolical and the meaning basically spiritual.

Then there are other passages like this one from Micah -

> In the last days, the mountain of the Lord's temple will be established as chief among the mountains;
> it will be raised above the hills, and peoples will stream to it.
> Many nations will come and say, 'Come, let us go up to the mountain of the Lord, and to the house of the God of Jacob.

He will teach us his ways, so that we may walk in his paths'.
The law will go out from Zion, the word of the Lord from Jerusalem...

(Micah 4:1ff)

Again, many people take this literally - and, of course, they may well be right! But it seems to me that if we do that, we have a serious problem. The New Testament teaches us clearly that the old covenant and the old laws have been superseded by the new covenant. And as we have seen, there does not seem to be a place for a rebuilt temple.

Should we not see this passage as a prophecy about the Church? The temple is the Church. It is, spiritually, 'chief among the mountains'. Peoples are streaming to it, as they have done for centuries. And the new law - the law of Christ - is going forth from 'Jerusalem', another synonym for the Church. So, too, is the word of the Lord. Such an interpretation is thoroughly consistent with the New Testament, and does not leave us with the problem of wondering how Old Testament law is to be imposed from Jerusalem, when Christ died to bring us into a new era of God's economy.

Another well known Old Testament passage is found in the book of Zechariah. The 12th chapter describes how Jerusalem will be a 'cup of reeling' for all nations and that when all the armies of the world are gathered against her, she will be 'an immovable rock' (vv 1-3). And so it goes on, with a description of how Jerusalem will triumph over her enemies.

Similarly, in the 14th chapter, Zechariah describes a graphic encounter between the forces of Christ and the nations of the world -

I will gather all the nations to Jerusalem to fight against it; the city will be captured, the houses ransacked and the women raped ... Then the Lord will go out and fight against those nations, as he fights in the day of battle. On that day his feet will stand on the Mount of Olives, east of Jerusalem, and the Mount of Olives will be split in two from east to west, forming a great valley, with half of the mountain moving north and half moving south ...

On that day living water will flow out from Jerusalem, half to the eastern sea and half to the western sea, in summer and winter. The Lord will be king over the whole earth. On that day there will be one Lord, and his name the only name.

(14:2ff)

It is very appealing to take this literally. And many people do so. The idea of the Lord fighting against the armies of the world and destroying them, and of Christ standing in power on the Mount of Olives, full of grandeur and dominion, while the mountain splits between His feet is an exciting one. I have heard people talk of Jerusalem becoming a sea-port (although the wharves would need to be pretty high as the city is 2,000 feet above sea level!)

Is it really right to think in these terms? Paul tells us that the weapons of our warfare are not physical, but spiritual (2 Corinthians 10:4). Could not this whole passage be a reference to the word of God triumphing over the forces of evil?

And could not the picture of Christ standing on the Mount of Olives be a reference even to His first coming? As a result, living water - real living water - of the kind that Jesus spoke about to the woman at the well, goes forth to both east and west bringing life wherever it goes.

It is interesting that Matthew takes two parts of this passage in Zechariah and applies them to the night of

Jesus' capture in Gethsemane! (Matthew 26:31 and Zechariah 13:7; Matthew 27:9 and Zechariah 11:12,13). This would suggest that the rest of it should be applied in the same way.

It is easy to ask questions. It is not so easy to give answers! And there is much more in these chapters that we should consider. Whatever interpretation we apply to the many prophecies about Israel must be consistent with the New Testament and the gospel of Christ.

For example, the first few verses of Isaiah chapter nine seem to have militant connotations, but the New Testament quotes them in reference to Christ's first coming (see Matthew 4:15ff). Similarly, Isaiah 42 talks about the nations coming under the law and justice of God, yet Matthew relates this to the earthly ministry of Jesus (see Matthew 12:15ff).

Further, it is interesting to see how often believers in Christ are described in terms that originally applied only to the nation of Israel.

The obvious example occurs at the end of the letter of Paul to the Galatians, where he describes Christian believers as 'the Israel of God' (Galatians 6:16). This is only one of two occasions on which the actual word 'Israel' is applied to Christians. However, the idea is present in many places.

The outstanding example is a passage from the book of Hosea where the prophet speaks of the restoration of the people of Israel -

> Yet the Israelites will be like the sand on the sea-shore, which cannot be measured or counted. In the place where it was said to them, 'You are not my people,' they will be called 'sons of the living God'...
> I will show my love to the one I called 'Not my loved one.' I will say to those called 'Not my

people,' 'You are my people'; and they will say, 'You are my God'.

(Hosea 1:10; 2:23)

In the context of this passage, Hosea seems to be talking quite directly of the nation of Israel. Banished into exile in both Assyria and Babylon, the tribes of Israel seemed to have been rejected by God. But, He says, I will still show them love and I will once again call them my people.

In the New Testament, however, this prophecy is clearly applied to the Church. Paul, for example, teaches that this is a reference to both Jews and Gentiles being called by God (Romans 9:23-26). Similarly, Peter, the other great apostle, says that Hosea's words have been fulfilled through Christ. In a letter addressed to both Jews and Gentiles, he writes, 'Once you were not a people, but now you are the people of God; once you had not received mercy, but now you have received mercy' (1 Peter 2:10).

Similarly, there is a powerful promise in the book of Amos which is applied in the New Testament to the Church -

In that day I will restore David's fallen tent.
I will repair its broken places,
restore its ruins,
and build it as it used to be,
so that they may possess the remnant of Edom
and all the nations that bear my name,
declares the Lord who will do these things.

(Amos 9:11,12)

This seems to be a strong statement of the restoration of the kingdom of Israel. However, James, the Lord's brother, takes this passage and quotes it as evidence of the Gentiles ('the nations') coming into the Church! (Acts 15:13-18).

The definitive passage is found in the letter of Paul to the Ephesians -

> Therefore, remember that formerly you who are called Gentiles by birth and called 'uncircumcised' by those who call themselves 'the circumcision' ... - remember that at that time you were separate from Christ, excluded from citizenship in Israel and foreigners to the covenants of the promise, without hope and without God in the world.
>
> But now in Christ Jesus you who once were far away have been brought near through the blood of Christ.
>
> For he himself is our peace, who has made the two one and has destroyed the barrier, the dividing wall of hostility, by abolishing in his flesh the law with its commandments and regulations. His purpose was to create in himself one new man out of the two, thus making peace, and in this one body to reconcile both of them to God through the cross, by which he put to death their hostility ...
>
> Consequently, you are no longer foreigners and aliens, but fellow-citizens with God's people and members of God's household, built on the foundation of the apostles and prophets, with Christ Jesus himself as the chief cornerstone. In him the whole building is joined together and rises to become a holy temple in the Lord. And in him you too are being built together to become a dwelling in which God lives by his Spirit.
>
> (Ephesians 2:11-22)

This crucial passage makes many vital points, but one thing comes through very clearly. In Christ, there is neither Jew nor Gentile, but rather 'one new man'. Once we were excluded from citizenship in Israel. We were foreigners to the covenants. But now, through the blood of Christ, this is no longer true. All who trust in him are now citizens in the kingdom of God.

This is not to say that all Gentiles who trust in Christ become Jews. Paul is careful to avoid this. What he does say is that in Christ both Jew and Gentile become the new people of God.

In Old Testament days, the people of Israel were God's chosen people. They were His elect in the world, called to fulfil His divine purposes. There is abundant evidence of this in the writings of people like Moses (Deuteronomy 7:7-9), Isaiah (eg 42:1;44:1) and Amos (3:2), to quote just a few.

In the New Testament, however, this role is clearly taken by the Church. There are literally scores of references to believers being variously called or chosen or predestined or elect to fulfil God's purposes. For example -

> For those who God foreknew he also predestined to be conformed to the likeness of his Son.
>
> (Romans 8:29)

> But we preach Christ crucified: a stumbling block to Jews and foolishness to Gentiles, but to those whom God has called, both Jews and Greeks, Christ the power of God and the wisdom of God.
>
> (1 Corinthians 1:23,24)

> For he chose us in him before the creation of the world to be holy and blameless in his sight. In love he predestined us ... In him we were also chosen, having been predestined according to the plan of him who works out everything in conformity with the purpose of his will, in order that we, who were the first to hope in Christ, might be for the praise of his glory.
>
> (Ephesians 1:4,11,12)

But you are a chosen people, a royal priesthood, a holy nation, a people belonging to God, that you may declare the praises of him who called you out of darkness into his wonderful light.

(1 Peter 2:9)

These few references are sufficient to make it plain that God's purposes now are being fulfilled through the Church, not a nation.

There are many who would agree with what I am arguing here to a point, but who would want to suggest that the two are not mutually exclusive. In other words, both Church and nation are the servants of God.

I think this is a reasonable point of view, and I would not want to dismiss it lightly. However, personally, I feel that the burden of the New Testament is that there is really only one people of God, and that since Calvary, these people are to be found in the Church.

The most difficult passage of all in this regard is in the letter of Paul to the Romans. In three chapters (9-11), Paul opens up the whole issue of the role of Israel as a nation. Regrettably, at least to us two millennia later, he seems to leave as many questions as answers. Advocates of all schools of thought seem to have found support for their opinions in this passage! So I hesitate even to comment on it! But I think that a couple of aspects need raising.

First of all, Paul begins the ninth chapter by making the clear point that God's people are to be defined in spiritual, not natural terms -

For not all who are descended from Israel are Israel. Nor because they are his descendants are they all Abraham's children ... It is not the natural children who are God's children, but it is the children of the promise who are regarded as Abraham's offspring.

(9:6-8)

To me, this statement seems cystal clear. God's people today are those who put their faith in Christ. There are many Jewish people today who are natural descendants of Abraham. But as to faith, they have none at all. I cannot see how these people can be considered the agents of God in the world. On the other hand, there are many Gentiles who are dedicated followers of Christ. Surely these are His tools on earth. (And, of course, the reverse is true in both cases.)

On the other hand, in the eleventh chapter, Paul says very clearly that God has not rejected His people. Like the branches of a tree they have been broken off, but they can be equally well grafted in again (11:19-23). However, this will only be 'if they do not persist in unbelief' (v.23). Indeed, this passage must be read in the light of the tenth chapter, which establishes beyond all doubt that only through faith and the confession of the Lordship of Christ can anyone be saved (Romans 10:9).

One little sentence in chapter 11 has been the cause of much debate, however. It is this - 'And so all Israel will be saved' (v.26). Furthermore, Paul goes on to say that 'God's gifts and his call are irrevocable' (v.29). Does this mean that in the long term every member of the nation of Israel is going to be saved anyway?

Obviously, this cannot be the case. Even in Paul's own day, Jewish people were told that if they did not repent and believe the gospel, they would perish (Acts 2:40; 13:40ff;18:6). Further, since that time, there have been plenty of Jews who have been sinful and wicked, just as there have been many sinful Gentiles.

They are all long since dead and can hardly be saved now! They all come equally under the judgement of God.

Similarly, at the end of the age, only those who trust in Christ will be saved, no matter who they are. So when Paul talks of 'all Israel' being saved, he must too be using the term in an all embracing sense to mean 'all of God's people'. In fact, just before he makes this statement, he talks about 'the full number of Gentiles' coming in. Coming into what? Evidently, the new Israel of God, the Church. So all Israel will be saved. But this 'Israel' will be composed only of true believers, redeemed through the blood of the Lord Jesus Christ. It is the same 'Israel of God' that Paul mentions in his letter to the Galatians (6:16).

We could go into this subject in much greater detail. But enough has been said at this point. In summary, I believe that God's people today are those who believe in Jesus Christ as Saviour and confess Him as Lord. All that the Scripture says about God's divine purposes applies to the Church. The passages about military conquest and the like actually describe the victories of the word of God in a sinful world (cf Revelation 19:13ff). The Old Testament's promises about the glory of Israel are seen in the beauty of the gospel.

Israel does have a place in the purposes of God - but not as a nation. God's true Israel is His Church.

9. What is the Millennium?

It is interesting that although the word 'millennium' nowhere occurs in the Bible, there are possibly more fundamental differences of opinion about this than about any other aspect of eschatology. There are three major schools of thought. These are premillennialism, postmillennialism and amillennialism.

A popular joke suggests that there is a fourth view - panmillennialism. This is the belief that 'it will all pan out in the end'. However, this is too easy an option!

The word 'millennium' is based on the Latin word for 'thousand' and means a period of one thousand years. Belief in a literal millennium at the end of the age is sometimes called chiliasm, a term based on the Greek word for 'thousand'.

The key biblical passage is Revelation chapter 20 -

> And I saw an angel coming down out of heaven, having a key to the Abyss and holding in his hand a great chain. He seized the dragon, that ancient serpent, who is the devil, or Satan, and bound him for a thousand years. He threw him into the Abyss, and locked and sealed it over him, to keep him from deceiving the nations anymore until the thousand years were ended. After that, he must be set free a short time.

The passage goes on to say that John sees the souls of those who have been beheaded 'because of their testimony for Jesus and because of the word of God'. Also, they have not received the mark of the Beast. They come to life and reign with Christ for a thousand years. The rest of the dead do not come to life till that period is ended.

At the end of the millennium, Satan is freed and leads the armies of the nations in battle. They surround 'the camp of God's people, the city he loves' but fire comes down from heaven and devours them.

Then follows the day of judgement in which all the dead stand before the great white throne of God.

First of all, let's look at the *premillennial* view of

this passage, which is the most popular view prevalent today. In simple terms, this is the concept that Jesus Christ returns to earth before the millennium and then reigns over the earth for a period of one thousand years. At the end of this period, the ultimate kingdom of God is ushered in.

Actually, its origins do go back a long way. (Of course, premillennialists believe its origins go back to the Bible itself!)

A very early comment is found in the letter of Barnabas, whose identity is uncertain. It is known, however, that he wrote around the end of the first century. He believed that human history would last just six thousand years and that the seventh thousand would be the millennium. In his view, five thousand years had already passed and the end of the age was not too distant (Epistle, 15).

Another second century writer named Papias believed that there would be a period of some thousand years after the resurrection of the dead, and that the kingdom of Christ would be 'set up in material form on this very earth' (Eusebius, *History*, 3, 39).

The esteemed Irenaeus seems to have endorsed Papias' view for he quotes it at some length, with embellishments (Against *Heresies*, 5, 33, 4).

Justin Martyr, who died in the way his name suggests in AD 165, once wrote a book called - *Dialogue with Trypho*, the record of a debate with a Jewish thinker in which he attempts to establish the authenticity of the Christian faith. At one point, he says -

> But I and others, who are right-minded Christians on all points, are assured that there will be a resurrection of the dead, and a thousand years in Jerusalem, which will then be built, adorned and

enlarged, as the prophets Ezekiel and Isaiah and others declare.

(80)

This statement is plain enough. And by implication it suggests that this was the standard view of Justin's day. However, this was soon to change. In Phrygia, a group of zealous Christians under the leadership of one Montanus, were attracting attention because of the strong emphasis they placed on both the charismata and the parousia. Whereas spiritual gifts were dying out in many places, here they were being earnestly promoted. Two prophetesses, in particular, were given a prominent role.

Moreover, they believed that the end of the age was upon them and that the Lord would soon return to establish a one thousand year reign over the earth. As it happened, they thought the Lord would return to Phrygia and daily looked for His appearing.

It should be added that the Montanists had many strengths as well. Their open testimony to the gospel, for example, can be strongly seen in epitaphs surviving from the third century - virtually the only part of the world where these are found, according to one historian (Chadwick, 1967, p.52).

Also, among their ranks was one of the early Church's most profound thinkers, Tertullian, who constantly argued for a genuinely spiritual approach to Christian ministry, rather than a hierarchical one.

Concerning the millennium, Tertullian wrote -
But we do confess that a kingdom is promised to us upon the earth, although before heaven, only in another state of existence; inasmuch as it will be after the resurrection for a thousand years in the divinely-built city of Jerusalem ... This both

210

Ezekiel had knowledge of and the apostle John be-
held.

(Against Marcion, 3, 25)

He goes on to say that a Montanist prophecy
actually predicted that there would be a vision of this
city in the sky to encourage believers, and that this had
occurred in Judea not long afterwards. Then he continues his explanation of the millennium, pointing out
that at the end of the thousand years, the world would
be destroyed and the saints would be removed to the
kingdom of heaven.

In spite of Tertullian's input, Montanist extremism
actually alienated the Church at large, and hastened
the conviction that spiritual gifts were no longer part
of God's economy. Montanism also precipitated a
wariness about chiliasm, and here, too, the Church became very cautious. So Eusebius, the fourth century
historian, is obviously not impressed when discussing
the views of Papias. 'He appears to have been of very
limited understanding,' he says (*History of the
Church*, 3, 39). In fact, for centuries, there seems to
be little evidence of any substantial teaching at all on
eschatology, and certainly, virtually nothing of a
literal or premillennial flavour.

The Anabaptists, the radicals of the Reformation,
were a bit like the Montanists. They had many fine
qualities and in the majority of cases were godly,
sincere, Bible-believing men and women. However,
there were some extremists among them, the most
notable example being the group at Munster who believed that their city would be the new Jerusalem.
Ultimately, under the leadership of Jan of Leyden,
they advocated polygamy and violence to achieve their
ends (Chadwick, 1972, pp.190f).

As far as other Reformation leaders were concerned, a belief in a literal millennium was a foreign notion. Calvin, for example, one of the Reformation's greatest thinkers, had only scorn for chiliasm. 'Their fiction,' he wrote, 'is too childish either to need or to be worth a refutation' (*Institutes,* 3, 25, 5).

During the seventeenth and eighteenth centuries, premillennialism began to grow in popularity again. According to J.W. Montgomery, 'virtually all the Christian leaders of colonial America maintained premillennialism: John Davenport; Samuel, Increase and Cotton Mather; Samuel Sewall; Timothy Dwight' (*The International Standard Bible Encyclopaedia,* 1986, Vol. 3, p.359).

It was only in the nineteenth century, however, that premillennialism again became a popular view. Most twentieth century evangelical and charismatic people are probably unaware of this because, at least until the 1980's, the only view presented in the majority of popular books on this subject was premillennialism.

It was a charismatic figure named Edward Irving (1792 - 1834) who began to popularise chiliasm in the mid-nineteenth century (Dallimore, 1983, pp.57ff). Irving, like the Montanists, also advocated the use of spiritual gifts, in particular prophecy, tongues and healing. And like the Montanists, Irving proved to be an extremist in both areas. In 1825, for example, he prophesied that the second coming would occur in 1864. Twelve apostles were appointed in the church and it was later believed that the Lord would return before the last of them died.

J.N. Darby (1800 - 1882), the founder of the Plymouth Brethren, was the man who really popularised premillennialism. He developed a view of spiritual history which became known as dispensationalism, which divided God's dealings with mankind into several dispensations. The result of his teaching 'quickened the expectation of the Lord's return' (Broadbent, 1985, p.379).

Darby's idea of dispensationalism was taken up by C.I. Scofield in his Reference Bible. Basically, Scofield describes seven dispensations - of innocence, of conscience, of civil government, of promise, of law, of grace and of kingdom. The last one occurs after the return of Christ.

The most popular presentation of premillennialism in recent years is to be found in Hal Lindsey's *Late, Great Planet Earth,* a book which became a run-away best seller. Lindsey's view can be summarised as follows -

1. There will be a literal one thousand year period at the end of the present age during which Christ will reign.

2. This period will be preceded by a time of tribulation.

3. The Church will be caught up from the earth out of the tribulation.

4. During the millennium, Satan will be bound and rendered ineffective.

5. Jerusalem will be the spiritual centre of the world which will live in peace.

6. There will be a final satanic rebellion after which the kingdom of heaven will be eternally established with a new heaven and a new earth.

7. Many Old Testament prophecies simply do not make sense if there is no such literal reign of Christ on earth. (Lindsey, 1971, pp.175ff).

It should be pointed out that not all premillennialists agree on all details. For example, historicists do not usually believe in a 'secret' rapture. They normally say that the Church will be caught up at the same time as Christ comes in judgement on the ungodly. Also, historicists believe that the tribulation covers the whole Church age, not just the last seven or three and a half years. In other respects, however, both historicists and futurists agree in their premillennial views.

The premillennial view also depends on a literal interpretation of many Old Testament passages. So prophecies about universal peace and prosperity (Isaiah 11:1ff; Micah 4:1ff; Zechariah 14:16ff; etc) are seen as literally being fulfilled during the millennium. For some writers, this is its strength. Erich Sauer, for instance, points out how many of the Old Testament prophecies were literally fulfilled at the first coming of Christ, and argues strongly that those prophecies which deal with the second advent must also be understood literally (Sauer, 1964, p.145ff).

The ramifications of such an approach, mean that Christ will reign visibly and personally on a throne at Jerusalem over an Israel restored to Palestine. During this time, people will live in mortal bodies, in ordinary houses, facing ordinary needs (Isaiah 65:20f). The temple and its sacrifices will be restored (Ezekiel 45:17) and circumcision will again be practised (Ezekiel 44:9). All the nations will regularly travel to Jerusalem to keep the feast of tabernacles (Zechariah 14:16).

For premillennialists, this is all acceptable. For others, there are real problems with such an approach - especially the reintroduction of a sacrificial system.

The second school of thought is *amillennialism*. This is really not well named. The Greek prefix 'a-' actually means 'not' (as in 'a-theist'). But amillennialists do believe in a millennium - it is the idea of a thousand year period at the end of the age that they reject. In simple terms, amilliennialists believe that we are in the millennium now. It is the gospel age.

The most powerful and influential presentation of this view in the writings of the Fathers may be found in Augustine's *City of God* (20, 7ff). No doubt partly in reaction to the extreme chiliasm of the second and third centuries, Augustine was also influenced by the reign of the Christian emperor Constantine, after whom a climate of peace and tolerance for the Church prevailed in Europe.

Basically, Augustine believed that the millennium was either the last of the sixth thousand years of history (which he believed were then current) or an indeterminate period of time, a view which he seemed to favour. He saw the number 1000 as a cube of ten and therefore suggestive of completion. During this period, Satan is bound in the way that Jesus described in Mark 3:27 and is cast into the abyss of the wicked hearts of the ungodly.

Meanwhile, believers are being born into God's kingdom ('the first resurrection') and the Church is reigning with Christ. Ultimately, Satan will be set free for a short time (three and a half years) and then finally destroyed.

Since Augustine's day, the amillennial view has been quietly held by many scholars and theologians. As we have seen, Eusebius, the historian, did not approve of premillennialism - his view was essentially amillennial. So was that of Jerome, the great Bible translator. (J.W. Montgomery in *The International Standard Bible Encyclopaedia*, 1986, Vol. 3, p. 358).

The Reformers were general amillennialists. The Reformation view is best summed up in the Larger Westminster Catechism where we read -

> We are to believe that at the last day there will be a general resurrection of the dead, both of the just and the unjust ...
> Immediately after the resurrection shall follow a general and final judgement of angels and men; the day and hour whereof no man knoweth, that all

may watch and pray, and be ever ready for the coming of the Lord.

(Questions 88 and 89)

There is no provision here for any intermediate period between the resurrection and the judgement day. It follows 'immediately'.

In more recent years, scholars such as W.W. Milligan, G. Vos, G.L. Murray, L. Berkhof and William Hendriksen, whose commentary on Revelation called *More Than Conquerors* is a classic, have all been amillennialists.

There are several fundamental precepts to amillennialism. One is that there are only two ages mentioned in Scripture - the present age and the age to come. Jesus spoke in this way when He warned that those who blasphemed the Holy Spirit would not be forgiven 'either in this age or in the age to come' (Matthew 12:32). On a more positive note, he declared that those who had suffered loss for His sake would receive a hundred times as much 'in this present age ... and in the age to come' (Mark 10:30).

Paul also referred to just two ages when He spoke of the exaltation of Christ (Ephesians 1:21). There is no room here for a third age - a millennium - to be slotted in between.

Furthermore, in his description of the return of Christ in his second letter to the Thessalonians, Paul describes all the godly as being saved and all the ungodly as being punished. What happens, then, during the millennium? What is the point?

Similarly, there is only one resurrection of the dead spoken of in Scripture and it takes place 'at the last trumpet' (Acts 24:15; John 5:28; 1 Corinthians 15:52). So when Revelation 20 talks of a first and second resurrection, there must be some other meaning intended.

This leads us to the basic concept behind the amillennial view which is essentially the conviction that the Apocalypse is written in symbolic language. Therefore, wherever possible, the symbolism should be discovered. The number 'one thousand', for example, is a symbolic number, as are the other numbers in the book of Revelation. It occurs some twenty times. It signifies a long period of time, but not necessarily a millennium.

Similarly, when the passage begins with a description of the binding of Satan, it is describing what happened after the resurrection of Christ. Note how graphic the description is. We have a vivid picture of an angel seizing Satan, chaining him and throwing him into the abyss! This is a scene of mastery and dominion.

Once when Jesus had just cast demons out of a blind man, he was accused of having done so by the power of Satan. To this, He gave a very logical reply -

> How can anyone enter a strong man's house and carry off his possessions unless he first ties up the strong man?

> (Matthew 12:29)

In other words, how can you cast out demons unless you have first restrained them and nullified their power? The message is plain. If you are going to overcome the devil, you first have to contain him. Jesus promised His disciples that this would be possible (Matthew 18:18).

In fact, it was accomplished through the cross and the empty tomb. Jesus rose from the dead and sat down at the right hand of God -

> far above all rule and authority, power and dominion, and every title that can be given, not only in the present age but also in the one to come. And God placed all things under his feet and

appointed him to be head over everything for the church, which is his body, the fulness of him who fills everything in every way.

(Ephesians 1:21ff)

In this great victory, Christ thoroughly defeated and demoralised and disarmed the principalities and powers of Satan's kingdom (Colossians 2:15).

So Satan's power is restricted and his weaponry removed. Believers now have authority over him (Luke 10:19) and can exercise dominion over him.

This gives a glorious sense of triumph to the followers of Christ. We are not living in defeatism. On the contrary, we have, through Christ, an incredible victory over the enemy! Jesus came, we are told, to destroy the works of the devil (1 John 3:8) and this He has surely done. We share in His victory.

Satan is unable to deceive the nations any more. This passage has puzzled commentators. W.J. Grier suggests that it has special reference only to Satan's ability to unite the nations in battle against the Church, for this is the very first thing that he does once the restraint is removed (Revelation 20:7). At the end of the age, then, as Paul describes it in 2 Thessalonians, there will be a fierce attack mounted on the people of God such as never seen before (Grier, 1976, p.114f).

The first resurrection mentioned in Revelation 20 actually refers to the new birth which the Scripture frequently describes as being raised with Christ -

As for you, you were dead in your transgressions and sins, in which you used to live when you followed the ways of this world and of the ruler of the kingdom of the air, the spirit who is now at work in those who are disobedient ...

But because of his great love for us, God, who is rich in mercy, made us alive with Christ ... and God raised us up with Christ and seated us with him in the heavenly realms in Christ Jesus, in order that in the coming ages he might show the incomparable riches of his grace, expressed in his kindness to us in Christ Jesus ...

(Ephesians 2:1ff; see also Galatians 2:20; Romans 6:1ff)

This powerful passage is not unlike the relevant verses in Revelation 20. If we remove the symbolism, we find that John is saying something very similar to Paul. In both cases, we have a picture of people entering new life and sharing in the sovereign rule of Christ. As a result, there is nothing to fear from the second death (Revelation 20:6).

In his letter to the Romans, Paul expresses a similar thought when he talks about 'reigning in life' (Romans 5:17). Already, it is God's intention that His people exercise victory over sin and evil and wickedness. In the beginning at Creation, He told the man and the woman He created to exercise mastery over the world in which He had placed them (Genesis 1:26ff). In Christ, that mastery is to be restored - not in a physical, but in a spiritual, sense.

Of course, the Lord Jesus Christ Himself is already King of kings and Lord of lords. Before His birth, it was prophesied that the Lord God would give to Him the throne of His father David (Luke 1:32). On the day of His resurrection, this promise was fulfilled (Acts 2:30.31).

Those who look for Him yet to come to claim His throne are looking in vain, for He has already inherited it. Of course, He is not yet enforcing or displaying all of its power, but that day will come.

A problem with this view seems to emerge when Revelation 20 talks of Satan being loosed for a little time (vv.7ff). If he is bound and conquered through the work of Calvary, how can this work be undone?

Augustine tried hard, but unconvincingly, to explain this, and eventually settled for a three and half year period during which Satan is released simply so that believers can see how powerful a foe the devil really is.

Another more helpful view is that the releasing of Satan is not to be taken chronologically at all, but rather to be understood as a way of explaining that even though Satan is bound, he still has a limited power which he attempts to use wherever possible. Certainly this is consistent with the rest of the New Testament which strongly teaches the absolute victory that our Lord Jesus Christ wrought over the devil, but yet at the same time warns us of Satan's wiles and his anger and his power. He is bound, but is still a deceiver trying to lead people into his snares.

Finally, the passage talks of the great white throne of judgement and the day when everyone, great and small, must stand before God (20:11ff). At this point, there is little difference between the millennial views. They all agree that there is a judgement day at the end of the age, and that we must all face our eternal destiny.

Until a few years ago, the *postmillennial* view was hardly heard of or known in the evangelical world. During the 1980's, however, it became popular once again.

In simple terms, postmillennialists believe that the present gospel age will introduce the millennium and that it will conclude with the return of Christ. The difference between this view and the amillennial view is twofold. First of all, postmillennialists do not necessarily believe that we are now in the millennium. They see it as a future golden age which will be brought about through the preaching of the gospel.

Secondly, postmillennialists see the gospel spreading more and more with its message of peace and hope and love until eventually the whole world is Christianised. On the other hand, amillennialists still see wickedness in the world at the parousia - indeed, perhaps even an unprecedented display of it.

A well known hymn expresses the postmillennial concept -

Jesus shall reign where e'r the sun
Doth his successive journeys run,
His kingdom spread from shore to shore,
Till moons shall wax and wane no more.

From north to south the princes meet
To pay their homage at His feet;
While western empires own their Lord,
And savage tribes attend His word.

(Isaac Watts, 1719)

Obviously, there are many similarities between amillennialism and postmillenialism. It is the positive thrust of postmillennialism which makes the difference.

It was Daniel Whitby (1638-1726) who inaugurated the postmillennial approach in the United States (Lovelace, 1979, p.408). Whitby, in spite of some heretical views (Pentecost, 1981, p.385) in turn influenced Philip Doddridge and Jonathan Edwards (1703-1758) whose ministry in the Great Awakening was so strong. A brilliant scholar and philosopher, Edwards believed that the Church would have such an impact that it would inaugurate a thousand year period of unparalleled blessing on earth. There would still be unbelievers, but these would finally be vanquished at the return of Christ. Here is part of Edwards' comment on Romans chapter 11 -

The Apostle, in the 11th of Romans, teaches us to look on that great outpouring of the Spirit, and ingathering of souls into Christ's kingdom, in those days, first of the Jews and then of the Gentiles, to be but as first-fruits of the intended harvest ... as a sign that all should in due time be gathered in ... the Apostle speaks of the fulness of both Jews and Gentiles ... These things plainly show that the time is coming when the whole world of mankind shall be brought into the church of Christ; the fulness of both, the whole lump ...

(Murray. 1987, p.296)

It will be evident already that Edwards' view of the millennium differed from that of both of the other schools. It was similar to amillennialism in that he believed Christ would return after the millennium. It was similar to premillennialism in that he did not believe that the millennium covered the whole gospel age. It differed from both in that he believed that the world would become Christianised through the preaching of the gospel.

John Wesley, too, seemed confident that the world would eventually be conquered by the word of God alone. In 1744, he preached to the staff at Oxford University on 'Scriptural Christianity'. Among other things, he said -

Can Satan cause the truth of God to fail, or His promises to be of none effect? If not, the time will come when Christianity will prevail over all, and cover the earth. Let us stand a little, and survey ... this strange sight, a Christian world. Of this the prophets of old inquired and searched diligently (1 Peter 1:10,11); of this the Spirit which was in them testified: 'It shall come to pass in the last days, that the mountain of the Lord's house shall be established in the top of the mountains ... and all nations shall flow unto it ...'

(Wesley, 1771, p. 43)

Wesley goes on to describe a world in which there is peace and unity; no noise of war is heard and nor is there crime or violence; indeed, even harsh words are not heard and every heart overflows with joy and praise.

Then he challenges his hearers for their part in all this. He urges them to total commitment to Christ so that they can set about this great task of Christianising the world! And in one delightful thrust, he hits home with, 'Let it not be said, that I speak here, as if all under your care were intended to be clergymen. Not so; I only speak as if they were all intended to be Christians' (p.48).

Postmillenialism became increasingly popular during the great days of the nineteenth century, when in both England and America, there were ongoing benefits from the revivals in both countries of the previous generations (the Wesleyan movement in England and the evangelical wakening in the US).

The Baptist theologian A.H. Strong presented the postmillennial view in his *Systematic Theology* (1907) as did Benjamin Warfield in 1929.

However, two world wars and universal unrest in the twentieth century did not encourage people to believe that there was a golden age for the church round the corner. Rather, it seemed that the only prospect for the future was despair and the only possiblity of escape in the rapture.

Many scholars continued to adhere to postmillennialism, however. In spite of the claims of some writers that it died out altogether by the mid-twentieth century (Pentecost, 1958, p.386; Lindsey 1974, p.164), in recent years, there has been a strong return to it, together with an accompanying defection from premillennialism.

In the United States, for instance, in the 1980's, the Reconstructionist school of thought, who talked about 'dominion theology' were attracting wide attention. Leaders in the movement were people like R.J. Rushdoony and Gary North, both of whom taught and wrote on a wide-ranging number of issues, but whose eschatology was basically postmillennial. David Chilton, an associate of North's, wrote a book called *Paradise Restored: A Biblical Theology of Dominion*. In it, he argues that God's original intention was that men and women should have dominion over the earth. This intention was restored in Christ. As Jesus Christ is now King of kings and Lord of lords, then it is possible for those who trust Him to exercise that dominion.

Hence, Chilton sees Christians gaining more and more sway over nature and over the world in general. Ultimately, the world will be increasingly Christianised. Not everyone will come to Christ, but even those who don't will be affected by the gospel. In this way, the world will be prepared for the parousia.

One major contrast between pre- and postmillennialism lies in the latter's sense of history. Most premillennialists live in almost daily expectation of the Lord's return. At its worst, this has militated against long-term planning. I personally know of people who have failed to buy a house, or to train for a career because they did not think there would be time to do so before the rapture. At its best, premillennialism promotes a sense of urgency to get as much done as possible while there is still time!

Postmillennialists, on the other hand, take a long-term view. To them, we might still be in the days of the early church. There could be thousands of years of human history yet before the end of the age. Long-range planning is part of the programme.

Christ must reign until He has put all His enemies under His feet (1 Corinthians 15:25). Increasingly, the dominion of the Messiah will be exercised until the whole world acknowledges His lordship. He is now King. He is now Lord. And this will eventually be realised in its fullest sense.

'We do not understand how anyone can take a long range view of history and deny that across the centuries there has been, and continues to be, great progress, and that the trend is definitely toward a better world' writes Boettner (1958, p.136). There may have been both advances and retreats, but eventually, the gospel must triumph!

The proclamation of the gospel and the ultimate conversion of a large majority of mankind was the express thrust of the Great Commission. Jesus told us to make disciples of all nations (Matthew 28:19,20). Did He tell us to do what we cannot do? Or did He expect this to be done?

In fact, the history of the early church shows that it is possible, for within four centuries, the whole known world named the name of Christ. If it could be done once, it can be done again.

Jesus called us to be triumphant. As Satan is bound, so the word of God is free! (2 Timothy 2:9). It can go forward in power to touch the whole world.

One of the problems with premillennialism, especially the futuristic variety, has been its escapist mentality. The world is growing worse and worse. Antichrist is about to appear. But there is no need to worry. Cheer up. Before things get too tough, the Lord will return and we'll all be celebrating in heaven.

Both of the other schools of thought share a much more positive, responsible, victorious approach. It is here and now that we are to see the triumph of the cross. Satan is now defeated. The victory is now ours!

Postmillennialism probably goes too far in its failure to come to grips with the fact that Jesus told us that both wheat and weeds would grow together and that unless the days of trouble are cut short, only a few will be saved. Similarly, Paul's teaching about the Antichrist points to a strong rebellion against the kingdom of Christ before the Lord returns (2 Thessalonians 2:1ff).

MILLENNIUM

'1000 YEAR REIGN OF CHRIST'. . .
(Rev. 20:1-10)

AMILLENNIAL VIEW. . .

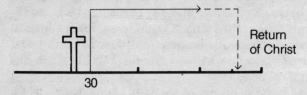

PREMILLENNIAL VIEW. . .

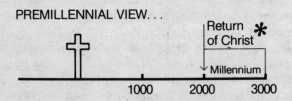

POSTMILLENNIAL VIEW. . .

In this respect the amillennial view seems to do most justice to the overall teaching of the New Testament. Certainly, it speaks not only of future victory but of the present victory of Christ as well.

Now, let's try to draw some conclusions. First of all, this is clearly an area where there is room for differing interpretations. We are wise if we keep a light touch on whichever view we favour. First of all, godly men and women may be found in all schools of thought. So this is not a matter of spirituality or even orthodoxy. It is very wrong to question the integrity of another over an issue like millennialism.

Secondly, it is interesting that millennial views tend to reflect the prevailing historical scenario. For instance, in the days of early Rome, the idea of an imminent parousia followed by an era of peace after the rise of a fierce Antichrist was very plausible.

In Augustine's day, with universal peace already evident, it seemed the millennium had already begun.

In the days of the Reformers, the scene changed again. Now, with the papacy seemingly fulfilling the role of the Antichrist, the millennium was forgotten: what was important was dealing with the present apostasy.

By the eighteenth and nineteenth centuries, the progress of the gospel was so impressive through the nation-wide revivals that were being experienced everywhere, it seemed only a matter of time until the millennium was ushered in simply through the proclamation of the word of God.

The disillusionment of the twentieth century with its wars and revolutions brought about a resurgence of the view of the early Church - our only hope was the return of Christ. In more recent years, however, the pessimism that this view inculcated in turn brought about a reaction, perhaps coupled with a new sense of power and purpose through the charismatic renewal,

and the result has been a fresh look at both amillennialism and postmillennialism.

One of the interesting phenomena of the 1980's was
the number of premillennialists who were actually teaching postmillennialism without realising it! On several occasions, articles or sermons were presented by
people who held a strong premillennial view. Yet they
talked enthusiastically about the triumph of the gospel
throughout the world and the ultimate dominion of the
people of God!

Thirdly, each view has its strengths and weaknesses. As we have noted already, premillennialism
can infuse an escaptist mentality - but on the other
hand, it can also encourage a sense of urgency.
Amillennialism can lead to an over-spiritualising of
the Scriptures - but it can also promote an exciting
sense of present victory over Satan. Postmillennialism
can raise false hopes of universal godliness in a world
still fallen - but it can also create an exciting sense of
destiny and hope for the Church.

Maybe in some respects all three views are right!
The most important factor is to see that whatever
stance we adopt, we are consistent with all that the
New Testament teaches about salvation and the
kingdom of God. It is only in the whole counsel of
God that there is safety.

10. What is Armageddon?

If ever you visit Israel, you will probably see the
ancient fortress city of Megiddo. Its excavations are
some of the most interesting and easy-to-follow in the
Holy Land.

You can walk through an underground water tunnel

that was built three thousand years ago. You can look upon a huge pagan altar where human sacrifices may have been offered. You can see a small stone manger, perhaps like the one in which Jesus was laid. You can gaze into a huge grain storage bin. And you can stand on top of the hill of Megiddo and look across the valley of Jezreel, the site of many an ancient battle.

When you enter the excavation site, you see a large notice on which is printed part of this passage from the Bible -

> They are spirits of demons performing miraculous signs, and they go out to the kings of the whole world, to gather them for the battle on the great day of God Almighty ... Then they gathered the kings together to the place that in Hebrew is called Armageddon.

> (Revelation 16:14-16)

The name Armageddon means literally 'hill of Megiddo'. In biblical history, the surrounding country was a common field of war. Joshua conquered the city (Joshua 12:21). Barak fought there with the kings of Canaan (Judges 5:19). Solomon fortified it (1 Kings 9:15). Egyptian records show that Pharoah Shishak conquered it. King Ahaziah of Judah died there (2 Kings 9:27) as did King Josiah (2 Kings 23:29).

The nearby valley of Jezreel was an ideal battle area both because of its terrain and its strategic position (1 Samuel 29:1ff; 2 Kings 9:14ff). In fact, Jezreel became a synonym for vengeance after the actions of Jehu to destroy the house of Ahab (Hosea 1:4ff).

It is no wonder, then, that the seer of the Apocalypse names this place as the centre of a great cosmic battle between good and evil.

Before we proceed, it is also worth noting that this same battle is paralleled in other parts of the

Apocalypse. It is described in chapter 14 where Christ's return is depicted as a great day of harvest. The wicked are gathered like grapes and thown into 'the winepress of God's wrath' (14:19).

There is further detail in 19:11ff. Here we see a dramatic picture of the King of kings riding forth on a white horse with a sharp sword with which He smites the nations.

The Beast and all the kings of the earth gather together to make war with Him, but they are easily overcome. The Beast and the False Prophet are thrown into the lake of fire. The rest are killed by the sword.

Similarly, in Revelation chapter 20, Satan gathers the armies of the world and attempts to fight against the people of God, but fire comes out of heaven and devours them.

Likewise, the Old Testament prophets speak of it. Joel, for instance, tells how God will gather all nations into the valley of Jehoshaphat (3:2). This name simply means 'the Lord judges' and is evidently not a geographical location. However, it does seem to be a reference to Armageddon.

Joel continues -

Proclaim this among the nations:
Prepare for war!
Rouse the warriors!
Let all the fighting men draw near and attack.
Beat your plowshares into swords
and your pruning hooks into spears.
Let the weakling say, 'I am strong!'
Come quickly, all you nations from every side,
and assemble there.
Bring down your warriors, O Lord!

(Joel 3:9-11)

Joel continues calling the nations to the valley of Jehoshaphat and then goes on -

> There I will sit
> to judge the nations on every side.
> Swing the sickle,
> for the harvest is ripe.
> Come, trample the grapes,
> for the winepress is full
> and the vats overflow -
> so great is their wickedness!

(Joel 3:13)

The similarity between this passage and the wine-press image used in Revelation 14 is obvious. Joel then goes on to describe 'multitudes, multitudes in the valley of decision' and warns that the Day of the Lord is near.

Zechariah also speaks of a day when 'all the nations of the earth' will be gathered against Jerusalem (12:3). However, Jerusalem will be a cup that people will risk their lives to drink - it will send them all reeling in a drunken stupor. Moreover, she will be 'an immovable rock for all the nations' and all who try to move her will only injure themselves (12:2,3).

The leaders will be 'like a firepot in a wood pile' (v.6) and even those with little strength will do exploits.

> The feeblest among them will be like David and the house of David will be like God, like the Angel of the Lord going before them.

(v.8)

The result? God will 'destroy all the nations that attack Jerusalem' (v.9).

That this passage, too, is talking about Armageddon, is fairly obvious. It is also suggested by a reference to Megiddo in verse 11.

The clear emphasis in all of these stories is that of

the futility of trying to resist the purposes of God. Ultimately and easily, God has the final word. Indeed, His victory is so sudden and so decisive, that the battle is never actually engaged! It is all over before it even begins.

Time and time again, this theme is reiterated in the Revelation. Whenever the enemies of Christ try to assert themselves, He rides forth in majesty and utterly confounds them. This is the great message of the book. And this is why it has always encouraged people of every generation. No matter what happens, no matter how hopeless everything seems, no matter how feeble we may be, we know that the ultimate conquest is the Lord's. We overcome Satan by the blood of the Lamb and by the word of our testimony! (Revelation 12:11).

But how is the Armageddon story to be interpreted? *The most obvious interpretation is the literal one*. This means that when the Apocalypse describes the armies of mankind being assembled at Armageddon, it literally means that the ancient battle site of the hill of Megiddo is the focal point of the battle.

In other words, at the end of the age, there will be an actual war between the armies of men and the forces of God. During the great tribulation, the Beast has been in control on earth and the saints have been raptured to heaven where they have been enjoying the marriage supper of the Lamb (19:7ff).

Finally, the world marshalls its forces and attacks Jerusalem, using Megiddo as a focal point for coordination. The nation of Israel stands alone in its resistance to this attack.

Then, just when it seems that all is lost, the Lord emerges from heaven with the saints and smashes the satanic hosts.

Lindsey gives one of the most detailed descriptions

of the sequence of events (Lindsey, 1874, p.135 ff).

First of all, he sees a Jewish Antichrist ruling from Jerusalem which as 'true' Bible scholars all recognise will then be one of the richest nations on earth. The Russians will then invade the Middle East, sweeping through the Arab lands and then into Israel. God will not allow the Russians to defeat the Jews and thus annihilate them. Meanwhile Red China will marshall an army of 200 million men to attack the Antichrist. At the same time, a revived Roman empire prepares for a showdown in the Middle East against the Chinese (Revelation 16:13ff). The battle site is Armageddon.

Lindsey notes that it is unusual that a land battle should be fought in these days of nuclear warfare and acknowledges that the movement of 200 million troops is not easy, but suggests that even though all this is 'incredible' it will happen. The final battle will be so dreadful that 'blood will stand to the horses' bridles for a total distance of 200 miles northward and southward of Jerusalem (Revelation 14:20).'

The whole earth will ultimately be affected and its cities destroyed. At this point, Lindsey quotes freely from the Old Testament - but not always appropriately.

Finally, the Jews see the hand of the Lord in all this and turn to the Messiah. Then, the Lord returns.

There are other variations of the literal interpretation which could be mentioned. For instance, Foster, a historicist, sees Armageddon as a battle between forces led by Russian communism and the armies of Protestant, Anglo-Saxon nations led by Britain and the USA (Foster, 1977, p.94).

Foster has other points of difference. Historicists, for instance, don't envisage the Church as being raptured during this period.

Overall, however, there is a very common and

widespread belief that there will be a literal battle known as Armageddon before the end of the age. So much so that even in the secular realm, people who know nothing about the Bible talk about the possibility of an ultimate world war which they describe as Armageddon. The *Macquarie Dictionary,* for instance, defines the word like this: '1. The place where the final cataclysmic battle will be fought between the forces of good and evil, prophesied in the Bible to occur at the end of the world. 2. Any great crucial armed conflict.'

There are real problems with the literal view, of course. To take just one example, the idea of blood flowing for 300 kilometres at a depth of over a metre is clearly impossible. This has to be taken symbolically. And of course, there are other very obviously symbolic pictures - such as that of Christ riding a horse and having a sword coming out of His mouth. If these are metaphorical expressions, then there must be many others as well.

In general terms, however, the literal interpretation may be seen simply as a ranging of the forces of the nations, inspired by Satan, against the armies of Christ, whose victory is swift and assured.

However, it is helpful to remind ourselves that Revelation is a book of symbols, so it is more likely that the name is used to *symbolise* a cataclysmic battle rather than to locate it geographically. In terms of modern warfare, the area is so small that it could not contain an international conflict, in any case. At most, it could only be an ignition point. There is one symbolic interpretation, for instance, that sees Armageddon as having occured at the cross! (Fullam, 1980). All the forces of hell and humanity were ranged against Christ. However, in one telling blow - His resurrection - Jesus broke through into a dynamic and everlasting victory! This idea is hinted at in the key passage on this subject, Revelation 16 -

> Then they gathered the kings together to a place that in Hebrew is called Armageddon. The seventh angel poured out his bowl into the air, and out of the temple came a loud voice from the throne saying, 'It is done!'
>
> (16:16,17)

There are several interesting points here. First of all, this bowl is poured into the air - the realm of Satan (Ephesians 2:2).

Secondly, a voice comes 'from the temple', which indicates its divine source.

Thirdly, there is an obvious similarity between the words uttered by this voice and the words of Jesus on the cross when He cried, 'It is finished!' (John 19:30). The Greek verb is different in each case but the expression is similar and the meaning almost identical.

Did Armageddon occur at the cross? Was the greatest conflict ever known to history actually fought there? Was the greatest victory of all time accomplished at Calvary?

When we think about it, the most astonishing battles of history - whether those of Alexander or Caesar or Hannibal or Napoleon or Wellington - all pale into insignificance against the cosmic encounter that took place at Jerusalem nearly two millennia ago. On that day, the demonic hosts were brought to their knees and their power forever broken. Sin's chains were smashed. Darkness was banished and wickedness defused. For the first time in history, men and women could know the glorious freedom from sin, guilt, fear and judgement that only the blood-bought children of God enjoy! It was indeed a great day and a mighty victory.

The major objection to this viewpoint is a chronological one. It does not seem to fit in the order of events in the Apocalypse. If Revelation is seen, however, as a series of brilliant panoramas of the triumph of Christ through His people, without reference to a rigid chronology, it is an appealing, and certainly very Christian, idea.

An *alternative symbolic viewpoint* also sees the battle as spiritual, but as a battle still be to won. What if we consider Megiddo simply to be a metaphor for Christ's victory? (Henriksen, 1986, p.162ff). Certainly, the oldest references to it in the Bible speak in this way. First of all, Joshua conquered it. Secondly, Barak won a great and decisive battle in the vicinity (Judges 5:19).

Then, what if Jerusalem means the Church? In this case, we have a picture of an assault against the Church by antichristian forces.

What if the sword of victory represents the word of God? In this case, we have the word of the Lord going into the world and winning victory over sin and evil, as it has constantly done. And finally, it will be the word which brings down all of Christ's enemies.

Again, we have here a powerful and positive presentation of the gospel which is thoroughly consistent with the rest of the New Testament. In many places we are told not to use human weapons, nor to retaliate with physical violence (2 Corinthians 10:4; Matthew 5:38ff; Romans 12:14ff).

But we are told to wield the sword of the Spirit and to fight constantly against the devil and his evil ways (Ephesians 6:10ff). In this way, we continue to stand against sin and all that goes with it, and leave the ultimate victory and the ultimate judgement to the Lord.

Does this interpretation fit all the relevant passages? Basically, yes, it does. As with any interpretation, there are always difficulties in fitting every detail. But the overall theme is valid.

THREE VIEWS
OF ARMAGEDDON

① THE COSMIC CONFLICT
AT THE CROSS
'It is finished' (John 19:30)

THE VICTORY OF THE
WORD OF GOD
IN HISTORY
'Out of His mouth. . .
a sharp sword'
(Rev. 19:15a)

②

③ THE END-AGE TRIUMPH
OF THE ARMIES
OF HEAVEN
'It is done' (Rev. 16:17)

Of course, no one can be one hundred percent sure which view of Armageddon is correct until human history is ended and we can look back on it and see clearly what really happened! Meanwhile, however, whichever view we adopt, there is one universal and consistent theme - the theme of the supremacy of Christ!

If the literal view is the correct one, the great message is that Christ is the Victor! No matter how powerful the armies of the nations may seem to be, their strength is feeble when pitted against the omnipotence of the King of kings and the Lord of lords. He always rides forth in conquest.

If the idea that Armageddon took place at the cross is right, the message is still the same. What a great spur to our faith to know that at Calvary, Christ overcame everything that the enemy could throw against Him! And indeed, it was the greatest battle ever fought in time or eternity. No other victory has ever been won at such cost, nor achieved so great a result.

If Armageddon is simply a symbolic picture of the continuing struggle between the kingdom of light and the kingdom of darkness, how encouraging to know that whenever the demonic forces of hell are unleashed against the Church, the victory is already assured! We do not have to crawl through life, cowed and beaten. Christ calls us to follow Him to the halls of triumph. There may well be wounds and bruises and hardship and pain along the way. But the ultimate victory is ours.

Satan is defeated!

Demonic power has been broken!

Sin no longer rules over us! Defeatism is a thing of the past!

Despair is irrelevant!

Christ always leads us in triumph! (2 Corinthians 2:14)

We have authority over the devil's power (Luke 10:19).

We are more than conquerors! (Romans 8:37)

He gives us the victory! (1 Corinthians 15:57)

All things are under His feet! (Ephesians 1:22)

We are seated with Him in heavenly places (Ephesians 2:6).

We are inwardly strengthened with divine power (Ephesians 3:16).

In the light of all this, right here and now, we can enjoy a victorious life. When we are tempted, we can conquer the temptation. For no temptation is too much for us (1 Corinthians 10:13). When we are cast down, we can rise up again (Micah 7:8). When we are beset with doubt, we can break through into faith (1 John 5:4).

In practical terms, this means that God's will for us is that we live a positive, creative, valuable life. Too often, we have seen Christianity as a drudgery, and we have moaned our way along. But the great theme of eschatology is that in the end, Christ always wins! He never comes second! And neither do we. As we trust in Him, we go through on top.

Whether it be in fair weather or foul, in joy or in sorrow, in suffering or in health, in fellowship or in solitude, in poverty or in wealth, we can enjoy Christ's victory.

Through prayer, through reading of Scripture, through faith, through worship and through fellowship, we demonstrate the victory of Christ in every situation. Our words are always those of praise, not those of complaint. We confess the blessings that are ours in Christ, not the failings that are ours in ourselves.

We refuse to accept defeat and are satisfied only with victory.

In the great Christian classic, *The Pilgrim's Progress,* Bunyan (1628 - 1688) tells how his hero Christian is engaged in a fierce conflict with Apollyon, the devil. The battle is long and grim, but ultimately Christian triumphs. Indeed, he is almost overwhelmed and Apollyon is ready to deal a death blow, when Christian makes one last frantic clutch for his fallen sword and swings it with a shout of victory. So powerful is his rally, that Apollyon flees.

At this point, there are four lines of verse which epitomise the believer's success. They provide an inspiring conclusion to this section -

A more unequal Match can hardly be:
Christian must fight an Angel; but you see
The Valiant Man, by handling Sword and Shield,
Doth make him, tho' a Dragon, quit the field.

CONCLUSION

A patient teacher had just completed a detailed lecture in which he had outlined the various views of eschatology. He thought he had been unbiassed and objective and that he had covered the whole subject rather well.

Were there any questions, he asked the class. A young lady raised her hand. 'Sir,' she said, 'I just want to know what *we* believe.'

You may be feeling the same way by now. Having read all the various viewpoints in this volume, you may be wondering what you really believe yourself. We have tried to be helpful by dividing the book into two parts. The first covers those areas on which most Christians are agreed. The second deals with more controversial issues.

Furthermore, in the second part, I have tried to cover the various views, but at the same time I have not tried to hide my own opinions. So if you agree with my arguments, there you have it!

In this whole area, however, there is great need for a generous caution. One man once said to a friend of mine, 'Well, you can believe what you like, but as far as I'm concerned, I'll just believe the Bible.' A fine-sounding sentiment, but really just an expression of the man's own bias and ignorance.

Here are a few concluding thoughts that might prove helpful.

1. *Whatever view we adopt, we should avoid dogmatism.*

Many wise and godly people have studied the same passages in the Bible and come up with differing interpretations. It is obvious that they cannot all be right. Yet they may not all be wrong, either. Everyone may have particular insights that are really helpful.

Imagine four theologians sitting in a library one day, when a pigeon flutters down and lands on the window sill. 'Aha,' says one, 'a symbol of peace.'

'No,' suggests another. 'In Scripture, the dove is always a symbol of the Holy Spirit.'

'Not always,' interjects the third scholar. 'It reminds me of the freedom we have in Christ.'

'I cannot agree with any of you,' argues the fourth. 'That bird obviously reminds us of the return of Christ.'

Now, so far, there is no problem. Each man has a perfect right to his view and each may have good reason for it. But let us imagine that this is what happens next -

The fourth man goes on to say, 'Listen, you may not agree, but I'm telling you that you are all wrong. There is only one possible significance in the landing of that bird. It is the message of the parousia!'

Another then says, 'Wait a minute! I have had such an experience of liberation in Christ that there can be no other meaning for me than spiritual freedom. That bird has nothing whatever to do with some eschatalogical event!'

And then the second speaker chips in. 'You men obviously know nothing whatever of the Scriptures. The dove is the outstanding sign of the Spirit. To say anything else is to border on heresy! I insist that you consider my viewpoint and that you seriously question your own views.'

And then the one who spoke first says, 'Listen to me, all of you. From time immemorial, the dove has been a sign of peace. I have history and tradition on my side. And I'm prepared to fight anyone to prove it!'

The problem is easy to identify. Not that they hold differing ideas, but that they refuse to accept each other's right to do so. As Jesus once warned us, sometimes the children of this world are wiser than the children of light in this regard. Voltaire, an atheistic philospher once said, 'I disapprove of what you say, but I will defend to the death your right to say it.'

We need a similar attitude in the area of eschatology.

2. *Treat all views on prophecy cautiously.*

As in all areas, there are both good and bad books on this subject. (You can judge for yourself which category this one falls into!) However, eschatology seems to be an area where the bad ones multiply like Joel's locusts. Much of the imagery in the Apocalypse, in particular, is of such a nature that the fertile imagination can do incredible things with it!

Unfortunately, most people are not very discerning in this area. If it sounds interesting and exciting, they will go for it! Recently, I was in a congregation of premillennialists who were being addressed by a very inspirational speaker who was, in fact, presenting a partly postmillennial approach! However, because he did not name it as such, and because he was so positive and enthusiastic, the audience loved it! They did not stop to think whether it was consistent with either the Scripture (which it basically was) or with their own traditional view (which it basically wasn't!).

In this case, no harm was done. But there have been cases of severe damage being caused to the whole area of eschatology through foolish predictions and interpretations. For example, in 1982, there were widespread reports that there would be a certain alignment of the planets which would result in severe earth-quakes, international strife and turmoil - all sure signs of the imminence of the parousia.

At that time, the assistant editor of *New Day,* a magazine I was editing, happened to have been a former secretary of the local astronomical society. So he researched the whole matter and found that the story had no foundation at all. We went into print to this effect. 1982 came and went and nothing significant happened - except that there should have been plenty of red faces around.

Similarly, a book called *The Cosmic Conspiracy* was widely circulated in Australia in the early 1980's. It made many astounding claims, including that the return of Christ could not be any later than 1981. It spoke of a conspiracy to take over the world; of sinister influences among the founding fathers of the USA, and so on.

In its opening section, it actually denied the Trinity, which meant that no thinking Christian should ever have taken the rest of it seriously. But the latter parts were so exciting, that no one seemed to notice that.

Of course, the book is now discredited, but meanwhile tens of thousands of copies were sold and thousands of tapes were distributed.

There have been many other such stories - like the so-called 'Beast of Brussels' computer; the fraudulent claim that a Cape Kennedy computer had located Joshua's missing day; the misguided and malicious allegations that a certain well-known international company was funded by Satanists, and so on. Not all of these are related directly to eschatology, but all of them help to create an atmosphere in which eventually no one takes anything seriously any more. As with the boy who cried 'wolf' in Aesop's fable, when a true cry is heard, no one will heed it.

The power of the gospel is such that it does not need bolstering up with fanciful stories. It stands on its own merits. And this is certainly true of eschatology. The obvious central truths about the return of Christ are so thrilling, so wide-reaching, so cosmic, so universal, and so majestic, that they can be proclaimed forth-rightly without embarrassment or shame.

The Lord Jesus Christ is coming back to reign on the earth! That, in itself, is enough to cause us to lift up our hearts for joy.

3. *To understand eschatology, we need a good working knowledge of Scripture.*

It is easy to jump to conclusions about the parousia, without being fully aware of the totality of the Bible's teaching on the subject. Of course, it would be un-realistic to postpone holding any opinions until we were experts. On the other hand, it is unwise to be too dogmatic until we are reasonably well acquainted with the facts.

In this book, for instance, we have tried to look closely and systematically at the major biblical passages, rather than to jump from text to text haphazardly. This is a wise way to go.

It is important, for instance, to be well versed in Jesus' teaching on the subject, especially in Matthew 13, 24 and 25, Mark 13 and Luke 21. It is also essential to have a good look at Paul's two letters to the Thessalonians. Revelation, of course, is required reading.

Isaiah, Jeremiah, Ezekiel, Daniel and the Minor Prophets all have important things to say about God's great purpose for mankind, and it is important to be familiar with them, too. This latter task is the work of a lifetime! But it is an undertaking which is well worth while.

As far as the New Testament is concerned, most people do not realise how quickly a whole book can be read. The Apocalypse, for instance, can be read in one hour at the very most. The letters to the Thessalonians are in reality just that - letters, and fairly short ones to boot. Ten minutes is all that is needed for a quick reading.

The nature of these books requires earnest study, and that does take time. But any thoughtful person can become familiar with the overall contents of books like these with relatively little effort.

There is no substitute for a good working knowledge of the Bible. There would certainly be far less confusion and argument if we all knew the Scriptures better!

4. *We need to remember that the testimony of Jesus is the Spirit of prophecy.*

It is very easy in studying eschatology to become so preoccupied with times, seasons, numbers and details, that we forget the real point. The essence of prophecy is bearing witness to the Lord Jesus Christ. Wherever a scheme of eschatology does this, we cannot be too critical.

Unfortunately, sometimes people are so intrigued with the peripheral aspects, that they ignore the essence. For instance, an itinerant minister once suggested that the computer bar codes on food products were indicative of the coming mark of the Beast. The result was that people became hesitant about buying such products. Of course, they really weren't in a position to do anything else. So here they were, compelled by sheer economic necessity to purchase products that they thought carried sinister markings, beset by guilt. Rather than encouraging them, this kind of teaching just took their attention away from the real issues. This was getting into the 'shadows' and away from the 'substance' which is Christ (Colossians 2:17).

THE NATURE OF BIBLE PROPHECY

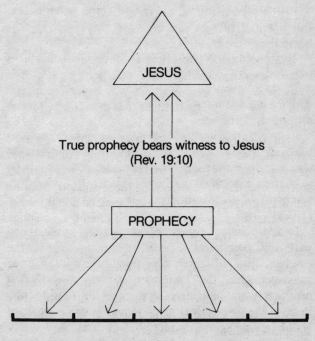

JESUS

True prophecy bears witness to Jesus
(Rev. 19:10)

PROPHECY

True prophecy speaks to all believers of
all time
2 Peter 1:19-21
1 Cor. 9:8-12
1 Cor. 10:11-13

The two great aims of eschatological teaching are holiness and hope. First of all, because of what is going to come upon the world, we must live holy lives, always ready for the return of the Lord (2 Peter 3:11ff; 1 John 2:28). We do not know the hour at which the Master will come back, so we must be living in such a way that whenever He comes, we will not be ashamed.

Secondly, in a darkening world, the only ultimate hope is the parousia (1 Thessalonians 4:13; 2 Peter 1:19). We know that the day will come when everything will finally be at peace and there will be true harmony on the earth.

The prevailing, consistent and universal theme of eschatology is the total, absolute victory of Christ. Whichever view we adopt and whichever interpretation we favour, the final message is the same: Christ is King!

In all of our preaching and teaching, this needs to be stressed. The morning I finished writing the first draft of my part of this book, I had risen very early in order to wrap up the final details of the manuscript before our staff prayer meeting. I was enthused about the exciting message of victory in which I had been soaking myself for weeks. I wanted to share some of it with the rest of our team.

Just before the prayer leader handed over to me, he suggested one more song. It began, 'Through our God we shall do valiantly ...' and finished with a three-fold repetition of, 'Christ is King! Christ is King! Christ is King!' It could hardly have been more relevant.

I hope that this message has come through in all that has been said so far. For this is the essence of the challenge of Christ's return.

What happens after the parousia is another story, certainly too much for this book. But we do know that there will be a new heaven and a new earth and the Lord will dwell among His people (Revelation 21:1ff; 22:1ff). There will be no more sorrow and no more pain.

And so we shall ever be with the Lord.

But you, brothers, are not in darkness so that this day should surprise you like a thief. You are all sons of the light and sons of the day. We do not belong to the night or to the darkness. So then let us not be like others who are asleep, but let us be alert and self-controlled ...

For God did not appoint us to suffer wrath, but to receive salvation through our Lord Jesus Christ. He died for us so that whether we are awake or asleep, we may live together with him. Therefore, encourage one another and build each other up, just as in fact you are doing.

(1 Thessalonians 5:4-11)

Bibliography

This is a list of reference books that Winkie and I have found helpful. Unfortunately, my office was gutted by fire a few months before I worked on this manuscript, and my library was largely destroyed. As a result, there were some books on this subject that I had read but which I have been unable to include in this listing.
Barry Chant

Recommended Reading

The following books are some of those I have found most useful in that they represent a balanced and biblical approach to the return of Christ.

William Barclay, *The Daily Study Bible: The Revelation of John* (Edinburgh: The St Andrew Press, 1976, 1985)

Geoffrey Bingham, *Revelation: A Commentary* (Blackwood: New Creation, no date)

Ken Chant, *The Return of Christ* (Sydney: Vision, no date)

D. Chilton, *The Days of Vengeance* (Fort Worth, Texas: Dominion Press, 1987)

R. Clouse (Ed), *The Meaning of the Millennium:* Four Views (Downers Grove: Inter Varsity Press, 1977)

W.J. Grier, *The Momentous Event* (Edinburgh: The Banner of Truth, 1945, 1976)

W. Griffin, *Endtime, the Domesday Catalogue* (New York: Collins, 1979)

William Hendriksen, *Israel in Prophecy* (Grand Rapids: Baker, 1974)

William Henriksen, *More Than Conquerors* (Grand Rapids: Baker, 1940, 1986)

William Hendriksen, *New Tesament Commentary* - 1 and 2 Thessalonians (Baker, 1955, 1974)

M. Inch, *Understanding Bible Prophecy* (New York: Harper and Row, 1977)

R.C.H. Lenski, *The Interpretation of St Paul's Epistles to the Colossians, to the Thessalonians, to Timothy, to Titus and to Philemon* (Minneapolis: Augsburg, 1964)

R.C.H. Lenski, *The Interpretation of St John's Revelation* (Minneapolis: Augsburg, 1961)

C.S. Lewis, *The Great Divorce* (Glasgow: Collins, 1946, 1986)

C.S. Lewis, *Mere Christianity* (Glasgow: Collins, 1952, 1986)

Robert Lightner, *Prophecy in the Ring* (Denver: Accent, 1976)

Richard Lovelace, *Dynamics of Spiritual Life* (Downers Grove: Inter Varsity Press, 1979)

R. Ludwigson, *A Survey of Bible Prophecy* (Grand Rapids: Zondervan, 1973)

Leon Morris, *The First and Second Epistles to the Thessalonians* (Grand Rapids: Eerdmans, 1973)

Leon Morris, *Revelation,* (Grand Rapids: Eerdmans, 1983)

Iain Murray, *The Puritan Hope* (Edinburgh: Banner of Truth Trust, 1984)

H.B. Swete, *The Apocalypse of St John* (Grand Rapids: Eerdmans, 1907)

Colin Weightman, *These Cry Wolf* (Blackwood: New Creation, 1981)

Reference Books

These are books from which we have drawn general information on all aspects of the subject.

Kenneth Barker (ed), *The Zondervan Study Bible* (Grand Rapids: Zondervan, 1985)

David Barrett, *World Christian Encyclopaedia* (Nairobi: Oxford University Press, 1982)

J. Sidlow Baxter, *Explore the Book* (London: Marshall, Morgan and Scott, 1952)

Louis Berkhof, *Systematic Theology* (Edinburgh: Banner of Truth, 1939, 1979)

Geoffrey Bromiley (Ed) *The International Standard Bible Encyclopaedia* (Grand Rapids: Eerdmans, Vol. 1, 1979; Vol 3, 1986)

B.H. Hall, *The Book of Daniel* in *The Wesleyan Bible Commentary* (Grand Rapids: Eeerdmans, 1969)

Henry Halley, *Halley's Bible Handbook* (Grand Rapids: Zondervan, 1927, 1965)

Everett Harrison (Ed) *Baker's Dictionary of Theology* (Grand Rapids: Baker, 1985)

Herbert Lockyer (Ed) *Nelson's Illustrated Bible Dictionary* (Nashville: Nelson, 1986)

James Moffatt, *The Revelation of St John the Divine* in *The Expositor's Greek Testament* (Grand Rapids: Eerdmans, 1967)

John Rasmussen, *The New American Revolution: The Dawning of the Technetronic Era* (New York: John Wiley 1972)

D.S. Russell, *Apocalyptic: Ancient and Modern* (London: SCM, 1978)

A.H. Strong, *Systematic Theology* (London: Pickering and Inglis, 1907, 1958)

Merrill Tenney (Ed) *The Zondervan Pictorial Encyclopaedia of the Bible* (Grand Rapids: Zondervan, 1982)

John Whitehead, *The Stealing of America* (Westchester, 111: Crossway, 1983)

Other Books on Eschatology

These books are quoted or referred to in the text and usually represent one particular point of view only.

Amillennian
Arthur Lewis, *The Dark Side of the Millennium* (Grand Rapids: Baker, 1980)
W.J. Grier, *The Momentous Event* (Edinburgh: Banner of Truth Trust, 1976)
Dale Tooley, *All Things New* (Wellington, N.Z.: published by the author)

Premillennial (Historicist)
Thomas Foster, *The Antichrist! Who Is He?* (Richmond: Published by the author, 1982)
Thomas Foster, *Great Pyramid Power* (Richmond: Published by the author, 1979)
Thomas Foster, *The Pope, Communism and the Coming New World* (Richmond: published by the author, 1977)
H. Grattan Guinness, *The Approaching End of the Age* (London: Hodder and Stoughton, 1880)
Leo Harris, *The Day Christ Returns* (Adelaide: Crusade, no date)
W.G. Hathaway, *Windows on Jerusalem* (London: Oliphants, 1969)
J.B. Nicklen, *The Great Tribulation* (London: Covenant, 1942)

Premillennial (Futurist)
Stan Deyo, *The Cosmic Conspiracy* (Perth, W.A.: W.A.T.T., 1978)

Salem Kirban, *Guide to Survival* (Melbourne: S.John Bacon, 1971)

Hal Lindsey, *The Late Great Planet Earth* (New York: Bantam, 1974)

Ernest Petree, *Approaching Events* (Osaka: Published by the author, no date)

Dwight Pentecost, *Things to Come* (Grand Rapids: Zondervan, 1981)

Derek Prince, *The Last Word on the Middle East* (Eastbourne: Kingsway, 1983)

Erich Sauer, *The Triumph of the Crucified* (Exeter: Paternoster, 1964)

Barry Smith, *Warning* (Palmerston North: Smith Family Publications, 1980)

Don Stanton, *Mystery 666* (Secunderabad: Maranatha, 1977)

Don Stanton, *Now and the Near Future Prophesied* (Secunderabad: Maranatha, 1978)

John Wesley White, *Re-entry* (Grand Rapids: Zondervan, 1971)

Postmillennial

David Chilton, *Paradise Restored:* A Biblical Theology of Dominion (Tyler: Reconstruction Press, 1984)

Gary North, *Backward Christian Soldiers* (Tyler: Institute for Christian Economics, 1986)

Historical Background

The following books have all provided interesting historical detail of the development of eschatology over the centuries.

A very long list could be included here, but basically only those referred to in the text are noted.

Primary Sources

Note that the writings of people like Irenaeus, Tertullian, Augustine and other Church Fathers may be found in the anthologies listed in this section.

John Calvin, *Institutes of the Christian Religion* (Philadelphia: The Westminster Press, 1559, tr. 1965)

J.B. Lightfoot (tr), *The Apostolic Fathers* (Grand Rapids: Baker, 1891, 1986)

Alexander Roberts, *The Anti-Nicene Fathers* (Grand Rapids; Eerdmans, 1979)

Philip Schaff (Ed) *The Nicene and Post-Nicene Fathers - First Series* (Grand Rapids: Eerdmans, 1979)

Philip Schaff and Henry Wace (Eds), *The Nicene and Post-Nicene Fathers - Second Series* (Grand Rapids: Eerdmans, 1979)

Maxwell Staniforth, *Early Christian Writings* (Harmondsworth: Penguin, 1982)

J. Stevenson, *A New Eusebius* (London: SPCK, 1960)

John Wesley, *Explanatory Notes on the New Testament* (Grand Rapids: Baker, 1986)

John Wesley, *Sermons on Several Occasions* (London; Methodist Publishing House, 1771)

The Westminster Standards (1648) (Philadelphia: Great Commission Publications, no date)

William Whiston (Tr), *Josephus, The Complete Works* (Grand Rapids: Kregel, 1969)

Secondary Sources
Roland Bainton, *Here I Stand* (Tring: Lion, 1984)

E.H. Broadbent, *The Pilgrim Church* (Basingstoke: Pickering, 1931, 1985)

Victor Budgen, *On Fire for God* (Welwyn: Evangelical Press, 1983)

Henry Chadwick, *The Early Church* (Harmondsworth: Penguin, 1984)

Henry Chadwick, *The Reformation* (Harmondsworth: Penguin, 1985)

Arnold Dallimore, *The Life of Edward Irving* (Edinburgh: Banner of Truth, 1983)

F.J. Dennett, *Europe: A History* (Melbourne: Linehan and Shrimpton, 1960)

Tim Dowley, *The History of Christianity* (Tring: Lion, 1977)

W. Haller, *The Rise of Puritanism* (New York: Harper, 1957)

Kenneth Latourette, *The Nineteenth Century Outside Europe* (Grand Rapids: Zondervan, 1969).

Elgin Moyer, *Who Was Who in Church History* (New Canaan: Keats, 1974)

Iain Murray, *Jonathan Edwards: A New Biography* (Edinburgh: Banner of Truth, 1987)

J.E. Orr, *The Light of the Nations* (London: Paternoster, 1965)

G. Parker, *The Morning Star* (London: Paternoster, 1965)

Philip Schaff, *History of the Christian Church* (Grand Rapids: Eerdmans, 1910, 1980)